Protection of Human Rights

Dr.Ravidankaur Rahul Karnani

Published by Amazone Kindle Publishing, 2018.

While every precaution has been taken in the preparation of this book, the publisher assumes no responsibility for errors or omissions, or for damages resulting from the use of the information contained herein.

PROTECTION OF HUMAN RIGHTS

First edition. February 26, 2018.

Copyright © 2018 Dr.Ravidankaur Rahul Karnani.

Written by Dr.Ravidankaur Rahul Karnani.

PREFACE

"The sacred rights of mankind are not to be rummaged for, among old parchments, or musty records. They are written, as with a sun beam in the whole volume of human nature, by the hand of divinity itself; and can never be erased or obscured by mortal power."

- <u>Alexander Hamilton</u>

In the progression of India, formation of the National Human Rights Commission is major step. It is well recognized that Human Rights form the foundations of a society and they are inviolable, as the society itself would disintegrate if they were violated. The society is formed to ensure through its laws, constitution and institutions that every one enjoys these rights. Thus, these rights must have a social respect and must be enforceable by the governments or other agencies who have the power to shape and influence the behaviour of others. The States, according to this perspective, derive their authority from the society to protect and safeguard these rights.

It is a vast subject which knows no limitations or boundaries. I have tried my level best to inculcate recent amendments and latest judicial trend so as to make the book a unique combination of law and practice. I hope this book entitled **'Protection of Human Rights'** will be very much useful for the students, academicians and even public in general. At last, I express a vote of thanks to all concerned and specifically my husband Dr.R.N.Karnani and my family for providing enormous amount of support without which present work was not possible.

(Dr.Ravidankaur R.Karnani)

TABLE OF CONTENT Page No.

Preface　　　　　　　　　　　　　　　　　　　　　　i

Chapter 1 Introduction

1. Protection of Human Rights　　　　　　　　　　　5
2. International Standards　　　　　　　　　　　　　8
3. Domestic Perspective　　　　　　　　　　　　　　24
4. Composition of the National Human Rights Commission 25
5. Definition of Human Rights　　　　　　　　　　　28
6. Complaint Handling Process　　　　　　　　　　　29
7. Power and Functions　　　　　　　　　　　　　　32
8. Paris Principles under the Domestic Legislation　　　34

Chapter 2 Civil and Political Rights

1. ICCPR, UDHR and the Constitution　　　　　　　42
2. Fake Enclunters　　　　　　　　　　　　　　　　45
3. Arbitrary Arrest and Detention　　　　　　　　　　48
4. Custodial Violence/Deaths　　　　　　　　　　　　50
5. Gujarat Riots　　　　　　　　　　　　　　　　　54
6. Harrasment of Undertrials　　　　　　　　　　　56

Chapter 3 Economic Social and Cultural Rights

1. Background　　　　　　　　　　　　　　　　　　59
2. International Efforts　　　　　　　　　　　　　　59
3. Constitutional Amendments　　　　　　　　　　　60
4. The Classification Error　　　　　　　　　　　　　61
5. ESCR under the UDHR and the Constitution　　　63

Chapter 4 Rights of Women

1. Right to Health　　　　　　　　　　　　　　　　74
2. Supervision over Protection/Cusotidial homes　　　75
3. Gender based violations/discriminations　　　　　　76
4. Trafficking　　　　　　　　　　　　　　　　　　78

5. Sexual Harassment	80
6. Rehabiliation of Destitued/margialiged women	81
7. Population Policy	82
8. Domestic Violence	83
9. Other Issues	83

Chapter 5 Rights of Child

1. Child Labor	85
2. Child Marriage	87
3. Child Trafficking	88
4. Sexual offences against child	89
5. Child Trafficking	90
6. Juvenile Justice	91
7. Other Issues	91

Chapter 6 Rights of Dalits

1. Rederessal of complaints	94
2. Eradication of Manual Scavenging	95
3. Rooting out Untochability	95
4. Working out with NGOs	97

Chapter 7 Rights of Underpriviledged Sections

1. Rights of Scheduled Tribes	99
2. Rights of the Disables	103
3. Internally Displaced Persons	107
4. Way Forward	110
BIBLIOGRAPHY	119
ACRONYMS	128

CHAPTER I
INTROUCTION

Respect for human rights is the hallmark of a civilised society. All human beings are born free and equal in dignity and rights. They are endowed with reason and conscience and should act towards one another in a spirit of brotherhood."[1] The sacred rights of mankind are not to be rummaged for, among old parchments, or musty records. They are written, as with a sun beam in the whole volume of human nature, by the hand of divinity itself; and can never be erased or obscured by mortal power.[2] Human rights consideration are relevant to almost every sphere to governmental activity and indeed, to many others areas of public and private life[3] as they are considered to be absolutely essential for ensuring the survival and a decent life to all human beings irrespective of their differences. Depending on the terminology adopted, they can also been referred to as natural rights, basic rights or even fundamental rights.

- **PROTECTION OF HUMAN RIGHTS**

There is wide agreement in the world today, especially among democracies, on the political significance of human rights. Every society creates legitimate authority that encompasses the relationships between its members and their relationship to the political authority. A civilised nation cannot ignore the violations of the human rights of its people. It must have effective systems for the prevention of such violations and for punishing the violators. There are different ways of protecting human rights. A pluralist and accountable parliament, an executive who is ultimately subject to authority of elected representatives and an independent judiciary are necessary, but not sufficient, institutional prerequisites.[4] Besides these basic 'institutions' there may be other mechanism called *'The National Human Rights Institutions'* whose establishment and strengthening will enhance the excising mechanisms. In many cases, the State is seen as a violator of human rights, and in other the State assumes the political responsibility to protect the rights of the vulnerable. This is increasingly being supplemented by a desire to provide for and devise appropriate human rights institutions.

The second half of the twentieth century saw the internationalization of human rights norms, which can be seen as the rationale behind the general notion that the protection of human rights is an international responsibility. However the recent proliferation of National Human Rights Institutions (NHRIs) show that the protection of human rights is not only an international responsibility but also a national one.[5] Their establishment is crucial to ensure monitoring and protection of human rights at the national level. Considering the above, a National Human Rights Institution could therefore be seen as a body whose functions are specifically defined in terms of the promotion and protection of human rights.[6] Therefore, any definition of what constitutes a NHRI must allow for broad, inclusive approach. Taking this into consideration, the United Nations (UN) has defined a National Human Rights Institution as a body that is established by a government under the constitution. By law or be decree, the functions of which are specifically defined in terms of the promotion and protection of human rights.[7]

Implementation of human rights instruments, and protection and promotion of human rights at the national level is a contemporary phenomenon that is still developing. The international norms of human rights are contained in the UDHR, 1948[8], the two covenants[9] and some international instruments[10]. But it is really difficult to find out what really constitutes a human right issue in developing countries where literacy rate is low and millions of people are illiterate[11]. Social backdrop of such countries is not conducive to practice of human rights as they are marked with endemic poverty, illiteracy, societal fragmentation and insensitive authority structure. As a result such countries are facing various burning human rights issues like- starvation, child labor, bonded labor, trafficking, rape and sexual harassment, custodial deaths and police excesses, fake encounters, domestic violence, honor killings, corruption, terrorism, involuntary disappearances, atrocities on Dalits/minorities, relief and rehabilitation of victims and many more. All in all this means that there is urgent need of effective mechanism that can promote and protect human rights.

At this juncture, the first and formost question arise is that an independent judiciary and democratically elected parliament are sufficient to ensure that human right abuses do not occur in the first place and therefore, the National Human Rights Institutions are not a wise use of scarce resources. In short, why the need for NHRIs when courts could address human rights issues? Some countries, for example the United States of America (USA) do not have NHRI's since they have effective courts and parliament which are adequate mechanisms for the promotion and protection of human rights. But than we may look at the case of Canada, where the presence of ethnic groups not being able to access court promoted the creation of a National Human Rights Commission as courts were seen as inadequate and a NHRC was seen as an adequate mechanism to protect the rights of these ethnic groups. The Studies have shown that the NHRIs have become instruments for the protection and promotion of fundamental human rights and freedoms.[12] Therefore, the effective enjoyment of human rights calls for the establishment of these institutions as they have an important and constructive role to play in the protection as well as promotion of human rights.

• INTERNATIONAL STANDARDS

For the National Human Rights institutions to promote and protect human rights effectively, it is necessary for a standard to exist, which relates to their functioning and by which such institutions will abide. A standard is relevant for reasons of uniformity and assessment of national institutions, especially with respect to the legal status of such institutions. At the international level, recognition of the contribution of NHRIs has become firmly entrenched during the decade of nintees. The creation of the International Co- ordination Committee of National Institutions in 1993, which comprises representatives of all regions, further emphasizes the importance of standards.[13] Due to the varying political context in which NHRIs are created there was an urgent need to set standard which such institutions should follow to ensure efficiency and legitimacy. This called for the need for international standards by which NHRIs have to conform. The result of which was the Paris Principles,[14] adopted in 1993 by the UN General Assembly. Consequently, many NHRIs have been set up on the basis of the Paris Principles. Even through the Paris Principles have been implemented mainly by third world countries and a few developed countries. It is however very important with respect to its legal status since it has been adopted by the UN General Assembly. Furthermore, the Vienna Declaration and Progreamme of Action adopted by the World Conference in 1993 encouraged the establishment of NHRIs and recongised the Paris Principles.The Paris Principles provide for institutional competence in the promotion and protection of human rights. In sum, the key criteria for NHRIs as laid down by the Paris Principles are: Independence guaranteed by statute or constitution; Autonomy from government; Pluralism, included in membership; A broad mandate based on universal human rights standards, Adequate powers of investigation and Sufficient resources.

Despite the increasingly expanding application of the Paris Principles, little is known regarding the origin and initial purpose of these standards. Moreover, a lack of awareness is apparent regarding the varying interpretations of the Paris Principles and the NHRI concept in current literature and practice. This Chapter will accordingly address: a short history of the 1978 NHRI concept and guidelines; the 1991 adoption of the Paris Principles and subsequent follow-up; and current applications of the Paris Principles and NHRIs in the international arena. Hence, there is need for a more precise understanding of the Paris Principles and NHRI concept, taking into account the nuances inherent to varying contexts of application. The Paris Principles set minimum conditions that a national human rights institution must meet to be considered credible by its peer institutions and by the UN. The Paris Principles require NHRIs to protect and promote human rights. More specifically, the Paris Principles set out six criteria that NHRIs should meet to be successful:

1. A broad mandate, based on universal human rights standards;
2. Autonomy from government;
3. Independence;
4. Pluralism;
5. Adequate resources; and
6. Adequate powers of investigation.

Principle 1: A Broad Mandate

The Paris Principles[15] provides that "a national institution shall be given as broad a mandate as possible, which shall be clearly set forth in a constitutional or legislative text, specifying its composition and its sphere of competence." The NHRI mandate must include the dual responsibility to both promote and protect human rights. Promotion includes measures such as public education, publishing reports, or taking other measures to ensure that individuals understand human rights standards and know that they must respect the rights of others. Protecting human rights means ensuring that there are effective mechanisms in place, such as investigating and monitoring human rights situations.

The Paris Principles describe the range of responsibilities that should be within the operational mandate of an institution as:

- Providing opinions, recommendations, proposals and reports to government, parliament or other responsible organs on: legislative or administrative provisions, as well as provisions relating to judicial organisations;
- the general situation of human rights or more specific human rights issues; and situations of violations in any part of the country.
- Encouraging the harmonisation of national legislation and practices with international human rights instruments, as well as their effective implementation;
- Encouraging the ratification and implementation of international human rights instruments;
- Contributing to country human rights reports, including, where necessary, by expressing an independent opinion on matters discussed in them;
- Cooperating with international and regional human rights organs, and other national institutions;
- Assisting and taking part in the development of education and research programmes in human rights; and
- Sensitising people on human rights and efforts to combat discrimination, especially racial discrimination, through publicity, information, education and the use of press organs.

With regard to the responsibility to provide "opinions, recommendations, proposals and reports", the Paris Principles make clear that an institution must, first, have the power to provide advice on its own initiative, and not merely on the request of the authorities. Second, an institution must be free to publicise its advice without restraint and without requiring prior approval. It should also be understood that the first responsibility listed (to provide advice on legislation and human rights violations and situation) generally includes the responsibility to:

- Receive, investigate and issue opinions and recommendations regarding alleged human rights violations (although it may not include the specific power to receive individual human rights complaints); and
- Monitor and report on human rights issues generally and on the situation of detained individuals in particular.

The Paris Principles do not say that the above-listed requirements are a definitive list of a NHRI's responsibilities; rather they constitute the minimum or basic level of responsibilities. That said, the Principles have not been interpreted as requiring that an institution actually carry out all of the listed responsibilities, but rather as requiring that there be no statutory or constitutional limitations that would prevent an institution from engaging in them if it chose to do so. An institution may, for strategic or resource-related reasons, determine to emphasise some responsibilities over others. Similarly, the implications of a broad mandate are that, subject to their statutes (as discussed in greater detail below), NHRIs should be directly engaged in work related to civil and political rights as well as economic, social and cultural rights. They may, within this broad mandate, however, choose to focus attention on one area, such as women's rights,[4][1] protecting the rights of persons with disabilities[5][2] and/or combating racial discrimination, depending on circumstances and priorities.

---

1. http://w02.unssc.org/free_resources/UNDP-OHCHRToolkit/chapter10/principle1.html#footnote4

Despite the principle in favour of a broad mandate, some restrictions are common and not problematic. For example, most NHRIs are prohibited from dealing with matters that are before the courts, or that have already been decided by the courts. Such limitations avoid duplication and the appearance of usurping the judiciary's role. They do not, moreover, contradict the Paris Principles. Many enabling laws specifically restrict subject-matter jurisdiction: for example, the NHRI may be authorised to receive complaints dealing with civil and political rights, but not economic, social and cultural rights. Similarly, some institutions have mandates that relate to one type of human rights violation – usually discrimination – but not others. Such limitations do not, in themselves, mean that the NHRI is not in conformity with the Paris Principles, but they should be read narrowly. In the examples cited here, a narrow reading would mean that restrictions that prevent the receipt of complaints in ESC rights should be read to be limited to complaints investigations, and should not diminish the institution's ability to comment more generally on human rights matters of all types, including ESC rights.

In other words, the NHRI should not be prevented from undertaking monitoring, public education or advice-giving in relation to rights for which it has no power to receive complaints. There are other types of restrictions: many institutions, for example, do not have jurisdiction to deal with human rights matters involving the private sector (companies and corporations). It is also true that some NHRIs cannot enquire into matters concerning the armed forces, the security services and/or government decisions regarding international relations. These restrictions do not contradict the letter of the Paris Principles, but they do contradict its spirit. Item 5.2 of the General Observations of the ICC[3] Subcommittee provide that "the scope of the mandate of many

---

2. http://w02.unssc.org/free_resources/UNDP-OHCHRToolkit/chapter10/principle1.html#footnote5

3. http://www.ohchr.org/en/countries/nhri/pages/nhrimain.aspx

National Institutions is restricted for national security reasons. While this tendency is not inherently contrary to the Paris Principles, it is noted that consideration must be given to ensuring that such restriction is not unreasonably or arbitrarily applied and is exercised under due process". It may be reasonable to place restrictions on who may access certain sensitive documents in cases where national security issues are demonstrably at stake, and where a judicial authority has proclaimed such to be the case, but wholesale exclusion of jurisdiction should be avoided.

Principle 2: Autonomy

The issue of autonomy is intrinsically linked to independence and is perhaps the most important of the principles elaborated in the Paris Principles[4]; it is also arguably the most difficult and controversial. In the final analysis, a NHRI is a state-sponsored body in the sense that its existence depends on an act of the State and on state funding: it is therefore accountable to elected representatives or to the government in terms of reporting on its performance, on the one hand, but is autonomous and independent on the other. Accountability to the State is generally achieved through annual reports and other types of reports filed with Ministers or, preferably, directly to Parliament. Interference by government in the activities of NHRIs is unacceptable.[16]

The dependence of NHRIs on government for funding may suggest that they cannot be truly autonomous. It is not unheard of for governments to restrict access to funding quietly – or to threaten to do so – when an NHRI is critical of the government's behaviour. More common is the unspoken pressure on a senior member whose career depends on the good will of the government. Despite these realities, it is possible for a state-funded entity to exercise autonomy: the courts, for example, are autonomous even though their funding comes from State coffers.

---

4. http://www2.ohchr.org/english/law/parisprinciples.htm

It is true that courts have a longer history, more structural guarantees of independence and are not administrative bodies, so there are important practical differences: nonetheless, the point here is that autonomy is possible. An institution's level of autonomy must be considered in light of a number of structural and procedural factors that should be in place to ensure a high degree of operational independence for an institution.

Principle 3: Independence

More than 70% of NHRI respondents to a OHCHR[5] survey considered their institution to be very independent in practical terms. While this is a positive indicator, a significant number of respondents also noted the influence of government departments or ministries over their budget allocation. As nearly half of the respondents in all regions (and slightly higher in Africa) indicated that their budget is insufficient, this administrative connection remains a problem area for many institutions.Although most NHRIs have legal procedures for the selection and appointment of the members of their governing body, these procedures need to be strengthened in all regions to include the public advertisements of vacancies (although this was notably more common in the Americas); the independent scrutiny of candidates, and consultations with civil society. In Africa, in particular, clear legal procedures for the dismissal of members are also frequently lacking."[17]

The Paris Principles[6] provide that an institution should have its "sphere of competence" set out in the constitutional provision or legislation that creates it and that it should have the authority to examine any human rights matter that is "within its jurisdiction". There are several reasons why it is important for an institution's mandate to be set out in a constitution or in legislation: it enhances the institution's permanence (since its mandate cannot be changed or withdrawn merely by executive order or, if there is a constitutional basis, even by law) and

---

5.   http://www.ohchr.org/EN/Pages/WelcomePage.aspx
6.   http://www2.ohchr.org/english/law/parisprinciples.htm

independence (since there is less fear of a changed or withdrawn mandate). Having a NHRI's mandate set out in legislation that has been approved by the nation's elected officials improves visibility and transparency. The public can refer to a text that sets out what that institution is meant to do, as well as what powers it has, and can measure an institution's performance against defined expectations. While the Paris Principles do not specify a preference for a constitutional mandate, having a mandate based in a constitution strengthens the NHRI since it provides more permanence (a constitution is harder to change) and gives the institution a higher profile in law. That being said, a constitutional mandate should be supplemented with enabling legislation that sets out in greater detail an institution's responsibilities, powers and authorities.

Independence is both operational and financial. The truest test of independence is found in the actions of the institution: an institution should have the ability to conduct its day-to-day affairs independently from any outside influence. This means that the institution has the authority to draft its own rules of procedure which cannot be modified by an external authority. An institution's recommendations, reports or decisions should not be subject to an external authority's approval or require their prior review. In terms of financial independence, the Paris Principles[7] require that funding be sufficient to allow the NHRI to have its own premises and staff "in order to be independent of government". The constitutional provision or law that establishes an NHRI should give the institution a separate legal personality sufficient to allow it to make decisions and undertake responsibilities independently. Having the institution report directly to Parliament or to the Head of State can diminish perceived interference that might exist if the institution reported to a Ministry.

---

7. http://www2.ohchr.org/english/law/parisprinciples.htm

The terms and conditions that govern appointment and dismissal of members should be transparent, i.e. set out in the constitutional provision or law (or both) that establish the NHRI. They should include:

- method of appointment;
- criteria for appointment (professional qualifications, recognised competencies, personal history of integrity and independence, etc.);
- duration or term of appointment and possibility of reappointment (guaranteed, fixed-term appointments, which may be renewable); and
- dismissal process (only for wrongdoing of a serious nature, clearly inappropriate conduct, serious incapacity. Mechanisms should be independent of the Executive, such as a Committee of Senior Judges, a court or a vote of Parliament).

The Paris Principles[8] emphasize the importance of the selection process of members, but not the ideal or required process. The following practices should be considered as practices that promote transparency and pluralism:

Explicitly including respect for pluralism and diversity as part of the selection criteria (see the next section);

- Involving Parliament in the formal selection process, by creating a short list of candidates, selecting candidates from a short list developed by the Executive, or formally ratifying decisions of the Executive; and
- Ensuring that social forces have a meaningful say in the process. This could be achieved through the establishment of a representative Committee of Experts to conduct the nomination and selection process. Alternatively, social forces

---

8. http://www2.ohchr.org/english/law/parisprinciples.htm

could be consulted directly to participate in nomination or short-listing decisions, perhaps by a Parliamentary Committee.

Principle 4: Pluralism

The ultimate purpose of pluralism is to ensure that the NHRI can establish 'effective cooperation' with other parts of government and society. Pluralism and diversity are important: they enhance an institution's independence, credibility and effectiveness; they increase the likelihood of cooperation and collaboration with other stakeholders, and they demonstrate that the institution itself takes equality seriously. One easy and effective way of doing this is to ensure diversity in the institution's membership, i.e. through diversity in its Commissioners or senior office holders. Where this is not possible, institutions can achieve pluralism through the use of advisory councils and other bodies that ensure broad-based input into their operations. In all cases, though, every effort should be made to support diversity in the institution itself so that management and staff reflect the diversity of a given society. The Paris Principles[9] require that "the composition of the national institution and the appointment of its members ... be established according to a procedure which affords all necessary guarantees to ensure ... pluralist representation" of representatives of all social forces engaged in promoting and protecting human rights. While the list of social forces or social actors set forward in the Principles also include Government, the Principles also make it clear that any Government official who is a member may only act in an advisory capacity so as to remove any suggestion that the institution is not completely independent.

It is not necessary and may not be feasible in countries with highly diverse populations to have each sector of society represented. However, the NHRI's, overall structure and, in particular, the composition

---

9. http://www2.ohchr.org/english/law/parisprinciples.htm

of its members, should facilitate cooperation and interaction with society as whole, and especially for vulnerable groups. While this section focuses largely on pluralism in membership, it should be remembered that pluralism can also be reflected in the work of the NHRI, for example: choice of trainers and participants for workshops, etc. and the thematic areas chosen for focus in research projects, seminars and in public education materials.

The ICC[10] Sub-Committee notes the critical importance of the selection and appointment process of the governing body in ensuring the pluralism and independence of the NHRI. In particular, the Sub-Committee emphasises the following factors:

a) A transparent process

b) Broad consultation throughout the selection and appointment process

c) Advertising vacancies broadly

d) Maximizing the number of potential candidates from a wide range of societal groups

e) Selecting members to serve in their own individual capacity rather than on behalf of the organisation they represent.[18]

While plurality is best demonstrated when an institution's membership visibly reflects the social forces at play in the State, this does not mean that all groups must be represented at any one time, but it should mean that, over time, groups feel that they are included. There are some basic factors that should be present as a matter of course:

- Plurality is easiest to achieve if an institution has a number of members;
- Institutions that have only one head or senior member, or very few members, can achieve plurality through the use of advisory councils or an equivalent mechanism;
- Women are always represented within the membership of an

---

10. http://www.ohchr.org/en/countries/nhri/pages/nhrimain.aspx

institution, including in senior positions;
- Where the structure of the organisation provides for only one member, consideration should be given to appointing women on an alternating basis; and
- In all circumstances, NHRI should collaborate and cooperate with other stakeholders, and doing so is itself a test of commitment to pluralism.

Plurality and diversity will be enhanced if staff composition also reflects societal realities. This means that diversity is reflected across all parts of the organization and all levels of seniority. Such pluralism can serve to enhance and strengthen the visibility of an institution's commitment to full participation, as well as positively influence programme credibility and effectiveness.

Principle 5: Adequate Resources

Financial autonomy is crucial. An institution with little or no control over its finances or its spending cannot be independent or autonomous. The source and nature of funding for an institution should be identified in the enabling law, which should guarantee, at a minimum, sufficient funding for the institution's basic functions. In some countries, an institution prepares its own budget, which it then submits directly to Parliament where the budget is defended. Parliament is then responsible for reviewing and approving the budgetary allotment as well as reviewing and evaluating financial reports submitted to justify the use of those funds. In other countries, it is the Minister with substantive responsibility for the NHRI that puts forward the budget. The first option, direct responsibility to Parliament, is the preferable scenario since it enhances independence.

The funding for an NHRI should also be 'secure', that is, it should not be altered arbitrarily during the period for which it was approved. This prevents a Government from penalising a NHRI for taking a decision or action that is critical of the government. Obviously, Parliament is the final authority on spending matters and, when faced with difficult financial circumstances, has both the duty and responsibility to oversee spending and to limit State spending if necessary. In such circumstances, at a minimum, a budget reduction should not be out of proportion to other core functions, especially in the area of rule of law.

Principle 6: Adequate Powers of Investigation

The Paris Principles[11] provide that an NHRI can consider any question, so long as it falls within its area of competence, whether it is submitted by Government or "on the proposal of its members or of any petitioner". NHRIs do not need the concurrence of a higher authority when deciding to consider a question. Furthermore, an NHRI operating in conformity with the Paris Principles will also have the authority to "hear any person and obtain any information and any document necessary" to examine such questions. The Principle that provides that an institution can consider questions on the proposal of a member or petitioner suggests that an institution should have the authority to hear from a victim, representatives of the victim or from third parties, and that it should have the authority to carry out own-motion investigations.

It is possible to have a Paris Principle-compliant NHRI that does not have the power to accept individual complaints. This is different from the general requirement in the Principles that NHRIs should have the power to protect rights. The authority to accept, and investigate specific complaints from individuals or groups is a specific and additional power. It is worth setting out the Methods of Operation section of the Paris Principles in this regard:

"Within the framework of its operation, the national institution shall:

a) Freely consider any question falling within its competence, whether they are submitted by the Government or taken up by it with-

---

11. http://www2.ohchr.org/english/law/parisprinciples.htm

out referral to a higher authority, on the proposal of its members or of any petitioner;

b) Hear any person and obtain any information and any document necessary for assessing situations falling within its competence".

The Principles provide that an institution shall consider questions on the proposal of a member or any petitioner. his suggests that an institution should have the authority to inquire into matters raised by a victim, representatives of the victim, or from third parties, and that it should have the authority to carry out own-motion inquiries. The additional Principles make clear that the authorities set out in the main body of the document also apply equally to institutions with quasi-jurisdictional authority. The Principles also state that NHRIs shall have the authority to "hear any person and obtain any information and any document necessary for assessing" the situation, presumably including when conducting inquiries or investigations. The authority to 'hear any person' implies that NHRIs should have powers to compel a person to give evidence or testimony and to protect individuals from potential retaliation for having done so. The authority to "obtain any information and any document" also implies that the institution has the authority to compel the production of documents and is able to use or access search and seizure powers, as well as to apply penalties to those refusing to produce, for destroying or for falsifying information and documents.

That being said, not all NHRIs have the specific authority in law to investigate individual complaints and this is not considered as making them non-compliant with the Paris Principles, so long as they do have the authority to inquire into matters or issues of a general nature. It is also true that not all NHRIs, including those with the authority to investigate individual cases, have the legal authorities and powers described above. This, too, does not mean that they do not comply with the Paris Principles. However, it is considered a 'best practice' that such powers are available to a NHRI since their absence reduces the NHRI's capacity to fulfil its mandate. Where they are available, it would be highly preferable if the founding law specifically provided the legal authority for this so that there is no doubt or confusion on the matter.

There exist a lot of questions regarding the substance and status of the Paris Principles. Firstly, the status of the Paris Principles has been an issue of debate, which reveals some doubts as to whether it is legally binding or not. In my view, the Paris Principles is not a treaty. Therefore, they are of the character of "soft law" and not "hard law" and thus have no legal forces. This explains why some NHRIs do not abide by the Paris Principles, as they are not bound by the Principles. Secondly considering the substance of the Paris Principles, it is obvious that the Principles, as has also been pointed out by the international Council on Human Rights, are inadequate in a some what paradoxical way. This is based on the premise that while the Paris Principles lay down standard to be met by NHRIs, it is surprising the some institutions have been effective in their own context without following the Paris Principles. That is, they had limited independence and inadequate funding yet have made a positive impact on the human rights situation in their countries.[19] But some institutions set in conformity with these Principles have been completely ineffective. This is because, although such institutions are established in conformity with the Paris Principles, the main reason for their establishment was to foster only the appearance of concern and to forestall domestic or international pressure or criticism. For example the creation of the NHRC was motivated by the desire to deflect criticism of the government's recalcitrance to political liberatsation.

Furthermore, the Paris Principles have shortcomings which allows the principles to appear to be noting more than normative standards. Firstly although the UN has classified an Ombudsman as a NHRI according to the Paris Principles, "the Ombudsman, mediators and similar institutions form other bodies" and are not defined as national institutions.[20] At least an Ombudsman plays a significant role in the promotion and protection of human rights and should therefore be regarded and treated as a national institution. Secondly, criteria for the appointment of members are too general, thus allowing for politically motivated appointments. This can only be prevented if the Paris Principles is more specific, and if the terms of appointment include a definition of method of appointment. Thirdly, although dismissal criteria have been elaborated in the UN handbook.[21] It would be more appropriate if it were also included in the Paris Principles. However, its worth noting that conforming to the Paris Principles are not always enough since this will not guarantee a resilient HRC without commissioner of integrity and a government committed to making respect of human rights a reality. In addition, although the Paris Principles appear to be nothing more than normative standard, but points of reference for setting up NHRIs.

The National Human Rights Commissions have been set up by many democracies as the most common and effective kind of National Human Rights Institutions. It is a multi-member institution set up almost everywhere with a role to protect and promote human rights and these are durable structures created by the State to redress various wrongs among people, wrongs created or perpetrated by socio-political institutions or those that reflect past practices. The National Human Rights Commission Model has become prominent actor in the national, regional and international human rights arena. The United Nations bodies and other funders in international donor community have directly encouraged and supported both technically[22] and financially its growth. The international community lends its support because it considers the process of establishing NHRCs to be an indication that a government is willing to abide by international human rights norms.

Thus, it can be seen that the central responsibility for protecting human rights rests with Governments. In recent decades, most countries have become parties to the major human rights treaties. Each instrument imposes legal obligations to implement, nationally, the human rights standards contained in those treaties. In ratifying an international human rights treaty, a State assumes the responsibility to respect, protect and fulfil the rights it contains. To respect means that the State cannot take any action or impose any measure that is contrary to the rights guaranteed by the treaty. To protect means that the State must take positive action to ensure that an individual is not denied his or her human rights. Mechanisms through which human rights are protected must be put in place. Adequate legislation, an independent judiciary, the enactment and enforcement of individual safeguards and remedies, and the establishment and strengthening of democratic institutions—all require State action. The responsibility to fulfil requires a State to take positive steps beyond mere prevention. This might, for example, go beyond the enactment of laws to promoting human rights through national education and information campaigns. When States ratify a human rights instrument, they have to ensure that the rights become part of or are recognized by the national legal system. States are required to take "all appropriate steps", including but not only legislative steps, to ensure that rights are realized at the State level. These steps are what is meant by "effective national implementation" and this has generated much international interest and action. The emergence or re-emergence of democratic rule in many countries has focused attention on the importance of democratic institutions like NHRIs as one of the key factors in implementing international obligations.

- **DOMESTIC PERSPECTIVE**

Incorporation of any right or rights to the citizens by the State is useless unless some protective and enforcing mechanism is provided by the State, for their implementation and protection. Keeping this in view, legislature while enacting any legislation simultaneously enact the provisions (or their protection and enforcement. The same position seems to be with the newly enacted Protection of Human Rights Act, 1993. It can also be said that the main objectives of The Protection of Human Rights Act, 1993 is to provide for the constitution of the

National and State Human Rights Commissions and Human Rights Courts for better protection of human rights and for matters connected therewith or incidental thereto. Thus, it has a twin objective to fulfill, namely, establishment of institutional structure, both at Centre and State levels, and to create enforcement machinery in terms of human rights courts for better protection of human rights.[23]

The Government of India did realise the need to establish an independent body for promotion and protection of human rights. The establishment of an autonomous National Human Rights Commission (Commission) by the Government of India reflects its commitment for effective implementation of human rights provisions under national and international instruments. The Commission is the first of its kind among the South Asian countries and also few among the National Human Rights institutions, which were established, in early 1990s. The Commission came into effect on 12 October 1993, by virtue of the Protection of Human Rights Act 1993. Twentyfour Indian States[24] have also set up their own human rights commissions to deal with violations from within their States. The Act contains broad provisions related with its function and powers, composition and other related aspects.[25]

- **COMPOSITION OF THE COMMISSION**

The National Human Rights Commission comprises of following executives:[26]

- A Chairperson, retired Chief Justice of India.
- One Member who is, or has been, a Judge of the Supreme Court of India.
- One Member who is, or has been, the Chief Justice of a High Court.
- Two Members to be appointed from among persons having

knowledge of, or practical experience in, matters relating to human rights.

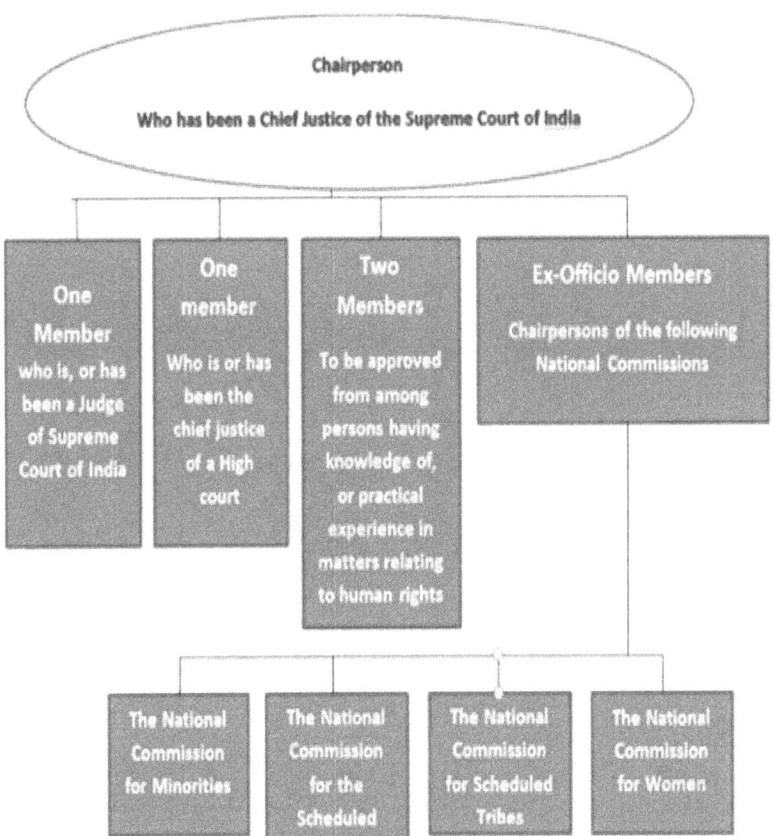

FIGURE 1:
Source: www.nhrc.nic.in

IN ORDER TO FACILITATE the work to the Commission, the Act also lays down that the Chairpersons of the National Commission for Minorities, the National Commission for the Scheduled Caste, Scheduled Tribes, and the National Commission for Women are to be deemed to be the Members of the Commission for the discharge of certain functions, except for function relating to inquiry into complaints of violation of human rights.[27]

Under the Act [28], the Chairperson and members of the Commission are appointed by the President of India on the basis of the recommendations of a committee comprising the Prime Minister, as the Chairperson, the Speaker of the Lok Sabha, the Home Minister, the Leaders of the Opposition in the Lok Sabba and Rajya Sabha, and the Deputy Chairman of the Rajya Sabha as members.

FIGURE 2:
SELECTION COMMITTEE FOR CHAIRMAN AND MEMBERS OF THE NATIONAL HUMAN RIGHTS COMMISSION OF INDIA

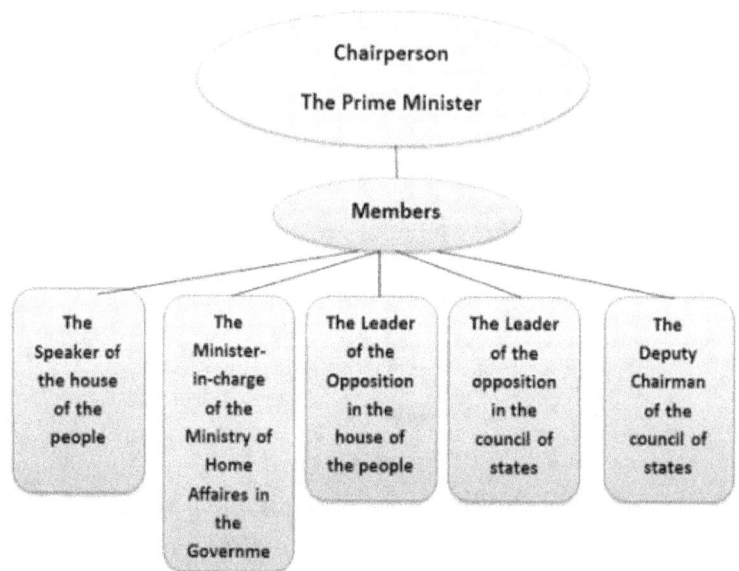

SOURCE:WWW.NHRC.NIC.in

The term of office of the Chairperson and members is five years from the date of assumption of office or until the age of 70 years, whichever is earlier. On ceasing to hold office, the Chairperson and members shall be ineligible for further appointment under the Government of India or under the Government of any State. In the event of the occurrence of any vacancy in the office of the Chairperson by reason of his death, resignation or otherwise, the President of India may, by notification, authorise one of the members to act as the Chairperson until the appointment of a new Chairperson to fill such vacancy. When the Chairperson is unable to discharge his Functions owing to absence on eave or otherwise, such one of the members as the President may, by notification, authorise in this behalf, shall discharge the functions of the Chairperson until the date on which the Chairperson resumes his duties. However, no sitting Judge of the Supreme Court or a sitting Chief Justice of a high Court shall be appointed without consultation with the Chief Justice of India.

- **DEFINITION OF HUMAN RIGHTS**

The Act[29] defines human rights as rights relating to life, equality and dignity of the individual guaranteed by Constitution or embodied in the international covenants and enforceable by Courts in India. The Indian Constitution provides certain rights for individuals in Part III of the Constitution, which are known as the fundamental rights. Part IV sets out the Directive Principles of State Policy[30]. While the former guarantees certain rights to the individual, the latter gives direction to the State to provide economic and social rights to its people in specified manner.

The word fundamental means that these rights are inherent in all the human beings and basic and essential for the individual. However, the rights guaranteed in the Constitution are required to be in conformity with the International Covenant on Civil and Political Rights and International Covenant on Economic. Social and Cultural Rights in view of the fact that India has become a party to these Covenants by ratifying them.[31] The justifiability of fundamental rights is itself guaranteed under the Indian Constitution.[32] The responsibility for the enforcement of the fundamental rights lies with the Supreme Court by virtue of Article 32 and by Article 226 to the High Courts.

- **COMPLAINT HANDLING PROCESS**

The Law Division of the Commission plays a pivotal role in both receiving of complaints and redressal procedure of such complaints of human rights. It also informs the petitioner and violative agency about the action taken or likely to be taken in that regard. The medium of interaction could, however be through any vernacular language as mentioned in Eighth schedule of the Constitution. However, no fee is chargeable on complaints. Presently, it is headed by a Registrar, one Joint Registrar one Deputy Registrar, 5 Assistant Registrars, 6 Section Officers, 9 Office Assistants and such other ministerial staff. The functioning of the Law Division of the Commission is quite systematic and meticulous. It acts in a sort of circle. First of all it receives the complaints and after formal registration of these it sends to decision-making body of the Commission. The decision-making bench, after a proper assessment of the complaint, passes orders having three different possibilities.[33]-

- Dismissal of complaint on the following grounds-

1. The complaints which do not fall within the purview of the Commission;

2. The matter is subjudice or pending before another commission;

3. The event which is the object of the complaint had occurred more than one year before making of the complaint;

4. The complaint which is vague anonymous or pseudonymous in nature; and

5. The complaint relating to service matter.

- Disposal of complaints with direction to the concerned authority where the case is to be decided.

- After the proper assessment of a complaint a notice is given, provided the Commission feels that the case comes within its purview and consequently detail reports are demanded from concerned authorities. In case of delays in furnishing the report, the Commission sends reminders 2nd then the concerned agencies/ authorities are bound to send the report to the Commission which passes the final order and sends the same back to the authority. However, all these works of the Commission are practically done by this division with the help of the computer-based network system.[34]

In practice, once the Commission receives a complaint, it categorieses the case in a particular head like-Custodial deaths; Police excesses (Torture, Illegal detention\ unlawful arrest, false implication); Fake encounters; Cases related to Women and Children; Atrocities on Dalits\Members of Minority community\ Disabled; Bonded labour; Armed forces\ para military forces; or Other important cases and than it seeks comments from the concerned government regarding complaint. After receiving the comments of the concerned authority, a detailed note on the merits of the case is prepared for the consideration of the Commission. After this, directions and recommendations of the Commission are communicated to the concerned government.[35]

The Commission while inquiring into complaints of violations of human rights may call for information or report the Central Government or any State government or any other authority or organization subordinate thereto, within such time as may be specified by it. If the information or report is not received within the time stipulated by the Commission, it may proceed to inquire into complaint on its own; on the other hand if, on receipt of information or report the Commission is satisfied that no further inquiry is required or that the required action has en initiated or taken by the concerned government or authority, it may not proceed with the complaint and inform the complainant accordingly.[36]

After completing inquiry, the Commission may take any of the following steps under Section 18 of this Act, namely:

- Where the inquiry discloses, the commission of violation of human rights or negligence in the prevention of violation of human rights by a public servant, it may recommend to the concerned Government or authority the initiation of proceedings for prosecution or such other action as the Commission may deem fit against the concerned person or persons.
- Approach the Supreme Court or the High Court concerned for such directions, orders or units as that Court may deem necessary.
- Recommend to the concerned government or authority for the grant of such immediate interim relief to the victim or the members of his family as the Commission may consider necessary subject to the provisions of clause
- Give a copy of the inquiry report to the petitioner or his representative.
- The Commission shall send a copy of its inquiry report together with its recommendations to the concerned government or authority who shall, within a period of one month, or such further time as the Commission may allow, forward its comments on the report, including the action taken or proposed to be taken thereon, to the Commission.
- The Commission shall publish its inquiry report together with the comments of the concerned government or authority, if any, and the action taken or proposed to be taken by the concerned government or authority on the recommendations of the Commission.

- **POWER OF INQUIRY AND INVESTIGATION**

PROTECTION OF HUMAN RIGHTS

The Commission is vested with the wide-ranging powers relating to inquiries and investigation under the Act. While inquiring into complaints under the Act, the Commission could exercise all the powers of a civil court trying a suit under the code of Civil Procedure, 1908 with respect of the Summoning and enforcing the attendance of witnesses and examining them on oath or Discovery and production of any document or Receiving evidence on affidavits or Requisitioning any public record or copy thereof from any court or office or Issuing commission for the examination of witnesses or documents; and or any other matter which may be prescribed. In order to discharge the aforesaid functions of the commission, certain procedures and regulations are followed by it. The Commission convenes its meeting at the discretion of Chairman and also regulates its own procedures.

FUNCTIONS OF THE COMMISSION

There are wide range of functions envisaged for the Commission under the Act[37]. These functions are:

(a) To inquire on its own initiative or on a petition presented to it by a victim or any persons on his behalf, into complaints of:

(i) Violation of human rights or abetment thereof or

(ii) Negligence in the prevention of such violation; by a public servant;

(b) To intervene in any proceeding involving any allegation of violation of human rights pending before a court, with the approval of such court;

(c) To visit, underintimation government any jail or any other institution under the control of the State government where persons are detained or lodged for purposes of treatment, reformation protection to study the living conditions of the inmates and make recommendations thereon;

(d) To review the safeguards provided by or under the Constitution or any law for the time being in force for the protection of human rights, and, recommend measures for their effective implementation;

(e) To review the factors, including acts of terrorism, that inhibit the enjoyment of human rights and recommend appropriate remedial measures;

(f) To study treaties and other international instruments on human rights and make recommendations for their effective implementation.

(g) To undertake and promote research in the field of human rights;

(h) To spread human rights literacy among various sections of the society arid promote awareness of the safeguards available for the protection of these rights through publications the media. Seminars and other available means.

(i) To encourage the efforts of non-governmental orgainisations and institutions working in the field of human rights; and

(j) To carry out such other functions as it may consider necessary for the promotion and protection of human rights.

- **STATE HUMAN RIGHTS COMMISSION AND HUMAN RIGHTS COURTS**

The National Human Rights Commission has urged all States and Union territories to constitute State Human Rights Commissions and notify a Court of Sessions to be a Human Right's Court in each district as envisaged by the Act[38]. Under a federal system such as ours, it is evident that a concrete responsibility must rest with individual States both to promote and protect human rights and to redress grievances. The decentralisation of the complaint disposal mechanism thus becomes a necessity, not least so as to provide a redressal mechanism that is readily accessible and inexpensive in terms of time and cost.[39] Following appeals by National Human Rights Commission and discussions with it, a number of States have decided to setup State Human Rights Commissions. At present, State Human Rights Commission exist in 24 States[40]. Accordingly in this chapter in attempt has been

PROTECTION OF HUMAN RIGHTS

made to study the perspective of State Human Rights Commission and specifically Rajasthan State Human Rights Commission.

Since, the enactment of the legislation, there have been bumps and potholes on the way in order to identify and overcome some of the structural deficiencies which impede the functioning of the National Human Rights Commission and State Human Rights Commissions. Domestic institutions like the State Commissions can play an important role in the effective implementation of human right standards at the State level. There is an urgent need to have closer interaction between the National Human Rights Commission and the State Human Rights Commissions as both are engaged in pursuit of the same objective-'better protection of human rights.[41]

- **Paris Principles under the Domestic Legislation**

To summarize, the extent to which the Paris Principles regarding the role and functions of the National Human Rights Institutions (NHRIs) have been incorporated in the domestic legislations of India, are summarised in below mentioned Table-

Table: International Standards Incorporated in the Statute Constituting the NHRC, India

S.No.	International Standards based on the Paris Principles	International Standards Incorporated in the legislations relating to the NHRC, India
1.	A human rights commission should be independent of the Government and its charter should reflect this. It should be established by law or preferably by a constitutional amendment.	NHRC was established under Section 3 of the Protection of Human Rights Act (PHR Act), 1993. Section 21 provides for setting of SHRCs in the States.
2.	Should consist of men and women known for their integrity and impartiality of judgement. The terms of their appointment, tenure and removal should be clearly specified and should afford the strongest possible guarantees of competence, impartiality and independence.	Sections 3, 4, 6 and 8 of the PHR Act, 1993, deal with the composition of the Commission, method of selection, tenure of appointment of its Chairperson and Members and terms and conditions of service of the Chairperson and Members respectively. The process of appointment however lacks transparency.
3.	Be mandated to monitor and report on compliance with and implementation of relevant international	Under Section 12(f), the Commission is empowered to study treaties and other international human rights instruments and make

	human rights standards.	recommendations for their effective implementation.
4.	Be mandated to review the effectiveness of existing legislation and/or administrative provisions in protecting human rights and should be able to make recommendations for the amendment of such legislation or introduction of new legislation as necessary.	Under Sections 12(d), the Commission can review safeguards provided by or under the Constitution or any law in force for the protection of human rights and recommend measures for their effective implementation.
5.	Establish effective cooperation with NGOs.	Under Section 12(i), the Commission is mandated to encourage the efforts of NGOs and institutions working in the field of human rights.
6.	Be empowered to investigate the conduct of police, the army and para-military security forces.	While under Section 12(a) the Commission can inquire into any violation of human rights or abetment or negligence in the prevention of such a violation by a public servant, in respect of 'armed forces' the powers are limited and the procedure prescribed in Section 19 is applicable.
7.	Should have its own investigative machinery and should have access to expert assistance	Section 14 provides that the Commission is authorised to utilise the services of any investigative agency of the central or state government. It

	whenever required, to verify alleged violations.	has its own investigation machinery as well.
8.	Should have powers to initiate investigations on its own motion and on omplaints or communications received.	Section 12(a) provides that the Commission can inquire suo-motu into any violation of human rights or abetment or negligence in the prevention of such a violation by a public servant.
9.	Should have full and effective powers to compel the attendance of witnesses and the production of documents.	Under Sections 13 and 14(2) the Commission has full powers to compel witnesses and production of documents.
10.	The result of the Commission's investigations should be referred to appropriate judicial bodies without any delay.	Section 18 provides the various steps after inquiry which the Commission may take, including approaching the Supreme Court and High Court for directions/orders
11.	Should have powers to ensure effective remedies including interim measures to protect the life and safety of an individual and free medical	Under Section 18(a) the Commission has only recommendatory powers. It can recommend to the concerned Government or authority, payment of compensation or damages to the victim or his family.

12. The Government should undertake an obligation to respond, within a reasonable time and publicly, to the specific case as well as to the more general finding, conclusions and recommendations made by the Commission.

treatment where necessary.

Section 18(e) provides that the Commission shall send a copy of its inquiry report together with its recommendations to the concerned Government or authority and the concerned Government or authority shall, within a period of one month or such other time as the Commission may allow, forward its comments on the report, including the action taken or proposed to be taken by the concerned Government or authority. Section 18(f) enables the Commission to publish its inquiry report together with the comments of the concerned Government or authority.

(2) Section 14 provides for the Commission to send its Annual Report to the Government. The Government, along with its action taken report on the recommendations, places it in Parliament.

THUS, IT IS WELL RECOGNIZED that Human Rights are the rights of the individuals, are recognized by the society and are to be compulsory ensured by the state. They form the foundations of a society and they are inviolable, as the society itself would disintegrate if they were violated. The society is formed to ensure through its laws, constitution and institutions that every one enjoys these rights. Thus, these rights must have a social respect and must be enforceable by the governments or other agencies who have the power to shape and influence the behaviour of others. The States, according to this perspective, derive their authority from the society to protect and safeguard these rights.

In the progression of India, formation of the National Human Rights is major step. It can play an important role in the articulation of human rights both, in the Indian context and at the international level. This Chapter brings out the relationship of NHRC with other relevant institutions engaged in the protection and promotion of human rights and how it can catalyse these institutions to work towards making the protection and ormotion of human rights a reality. Within the national system, the Commission is placed in a strategic position to influence all the key players in the protection and promotion of human rights as enviged in the OHCHR survey[42]-

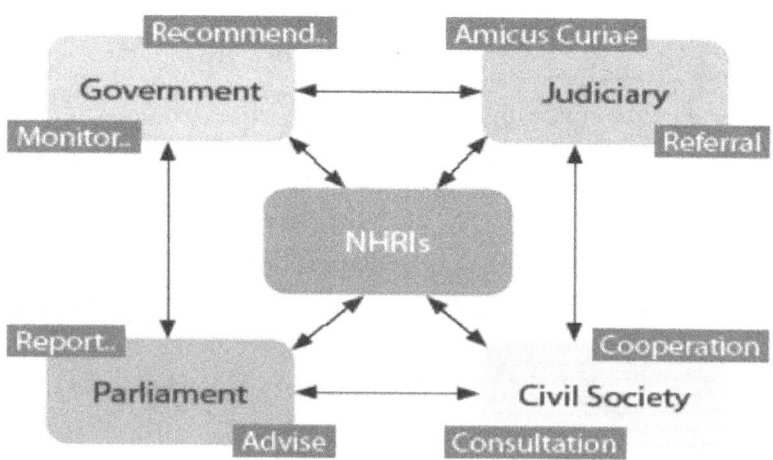

Source: National Institutions and Regional Mechanisms Section of the OHCHR

Thus, it can be seen that the statute establishing NHRC is largely modelled on international norms. But in practical terms, there are many limitations in the functioning of the NHRC. Some limitations stem from the weaknesses inherent in the constituent statute while some can be attributed to the reluctance on part of the Commission to act.Though the founding of the National Human Rights Commission is great step, yet sometimes it cannot perform its duties effectively. It does not have any independent mechanism of investigation. It always depends on the staff of the central and state governments. So its investigation sometimes fails to be unbiased. National Human Rights Commission can only make recommendations, without the power to impose decisions. This lack of authority to ensure compliance can lead to outright denial of its decision too. The law requires the NHRC to concentrate more on Civil and political than on social and educational rights. This is somewhat unfortunate as a human rights commission can really play an effective role in pressurizing the government to provide social and economic justice to citizen. Further, the Commission is supposed to be completely independent if its functioning, even though the Act doesn't say so. In fact, there are provisions in the act which underscores the dependence of the Commission of the Government. The National Human Rights Commission in India has effectively demonstrated its inclination to act as an effective organisation in the protection of Human Rights. In majority cases, it asks the concerned Central and State Governments to investigate the cases of the violation of Human Rights. It also approaches the Supreme Court and the High Courts to provide judicial assistance to the victims. But the structural deficiencies in the empowering Act of the National Human Rights Commission of India urgently needs to be solved out as quite often it is termed as "India's teasing illusion" or "toothless tiger" due to its incapacity to render any practical relief to the aggrieved party.

CHAPTER -II
CIVIL AND POLITICAL RIGHTS

In democratic societies, fundamental human rights are broadly classified into civil and political rights on the one hand and economic, social and cultural rights on the other. Civil and political rights are a class of rights that protect individuals' freedom from infringement by governments, social organizations, and private individuals. They ensure one's ability to participate in the civil and political life of the society and state without discrimination or repression.

In **Keshavananda Bhi'rati v. State of Kerela**,[43] the Supreme Court observed, "The Universal Declaration of Human Rights may not be a legally binding instrument but it shows how India understood the nature of human rights at the time the Constitution was adopted." In the case of **Jolly George Varghese v. Bank of Cochin'**,[44] the point involved was whether a right incorporated in the Covenant on Civil and Political Rights, which is not recognised in the Indian Constitution, shall be available to the individuals in India. Justice Krishna Iyer reiterated dualism and asserted that the positive commitment of the State Parties ignites legislative action at home but does not automatically make the Covenant an enforceable part of the 'Corpus Juris' in India. Thus, although the Supreme Court has stated that the Universal Declaration cannot create a binding set of rules and that even international treaties may at best inform judicial institutions and inspire legislative action. Constitutional interpretation in India has been strongly influenced by the Declaration.

Table 1 Civil and Political Rights in the Universal Declaration of Human Rights and in the Indian Constitution[45]

No.	Name of Right	The Universal Declaration of Human Rights	The Constitution of India
1	Equality before Law	Article 7	Article 14
2	Prohibition of Discrimination	Article 7	Article 15(1)
3	Equality of Opportunity	Article 21(2)	Article 16(1)
4	Freedom of Speech and Expression	Article 19	Article 19(1)(a)
5	Freedom of Peaceful Assemby	Article 20	Article 19(1)(b)
6	Right to Form association or Unions	Article 23(4)	Article 19(1)(c)
7	Freedom to move withing the boarder	Article 13(1)	Article 19(1)(d)
8	Protection in respect of conviction for offences	Article 11(2)	Article 20(1)
9	Protection of Life and Personal Liberty	Article 3	Article 21
10	Protection from slavery and forced labor	Article 4	Article 23
11	Freedom of conscience and religion	Article 18	Article 25(1)
12	Remedy for enforcement of rights	Article 8	Article 32
13	Rights against arbitrary arrest	Article 9	Article 22
14	Rights to social security	Article 22	Article 29(1)

India is a signatory to the Universal Declaration of Human Rights. A number of fundamental rigts guaranteed to the individuals in Part Ill of the lndian Constitution are similar to the provisions of the Universal Declaration of Human Rights. The following chart makes it very clear. In the judgement given in **the Chairman, Railway Board and others v. Mrs. Chandrima**[46], the Supreme Court observed that the Declaration has the international recognition as the Moral Code of Conduct having been adopted by the General Assembly of the United Nations. The applicability of the Universal Declaration of Human Rights and principles thereof may have to be read, if need be, into the domestic jurisprudence. In a number of cases the Declaration has been referred to in the decisions of the Supreme Court and State High Courts. lndia ratified the Interniational Covenant on Civil and Political Rights and the International Covenant on Economic, Social and Cultural Rights on March 27, 1979. The Optonal Protocol to the International Covenant on Civil and Political Rights, 1989, however, was not ratifled by lndia.

The Judicially enforceable fundamental rights, which encompass all seminal civil and political rights and some of the rights of the minorities, are enshrined in Part III of the constitution (Articles 12 to 35). These include the right to equality, the right to freedom, the right against exploitation, the right to freedom of religion, cultural, and educational rights, and the right to constitutional remedies. Fundamental rights differ from ordinary rights in the sense that the former are inviolable. No law, ordinance, custom, usage, or administrative order can abridge or take them away. Any law, which is violative of any of the fundamental right, is void. In **ADM Jabalpur v. Shukla,**[47] Justice Beg observed "the object of making certain general aspects of rights fundamental is to guarantee them against illegal invasion of these rights by executive, legislative, or judicial organ of the State." Earlier, Chief Justice Subba Rao in **Golak Nath v. State of punjab**[48] had rightly observed, "Fundamental rights are the modern name for what have been traditionally known as natural rights," The Supreme Court of India recognises these fundamental rights as 'Natural Rights' or 'Human Rights'. While referring to the fundamental rights contained in Part Ill of the Constitution, Sikri the then Chief Justice of the Supreme Court, in **Keshavananda Bharati v. State of Kerela**,[49] observed, "I am unable to hold these provisions to show that rights are not natural or inalienable rights. As a matter of fact India was a party to the Universal Declaration of Rights and that Declaration describes some fundamental rights as inalienable." The Chief Justice Patanjali Shastri in **State of West Bengal v. Subodh Gopal Bose**[50] referred to fundamental rights as those great and basic rights, which are recognised and guaranteed as the natural rights inherent in the status of a citizen of a free country.

But the Indian criminal justice system is adversarial and accusational in nature and draws inspiration from the common law system. Towering over society, it parades an array of institutions, processes, people and penalties to reinforce its image. This array includes policemen in uniform, constables with batons or lathis, the (police) station, courts, prisons and correctional agencies etc. Each of these institutions and processes is an integral part of the Criminal Justice System and yet partly autonomous within it. Together they represent a 'hegemonic' array of the power of the State to exact, respect, support and comply. At one extreme, the Criminal Justice System represents a public necessity to correct private and public wrongs firmly and fairly. While at the other extreme it may be turned into an apparatus of oppression and systematic abuse. In either case, we have been rightly reminded, the Criminal Justice System institutions and processes are expressions of State power, which sustain an ideological image of governance embedded in people's minds. Thus, the Criminal Justice System represents the cutting edge of governance. But Criminal procedure in India is fundamentally accusational i.e. although the procedure of a criminal trial is codified in the Criminal Procedure Code and the Indian Evidence Act, but it is no surprise that at various stages such as investigation of offence, prosecution and trial the norms are violated. All such instances of violation of the norms, which include abuse of power as well as non-exercise of power involves violation of human rights of the criminal or the victims. Thus, all the instances of violation of the norms also constitute acts of deviation from human rights standards.[51] The Commission has appraised such deviation particularly in the following instances:

(a) **Fake Encounters**

Encounter killings have been taking place all over the country over the years, at times degenerating into what are called fake encounters. Between 2000 and 2007 there have been 712 cases of police encounters in the country with UP topping the list at 324, and Gujarat figuring almost at the bottom with 17.[52] During 2015-16 the maximum number of complaints (32,498) were registered against the police, out of which 206 cases were encounters. Chhattisgarh with 66 encounter cases, topped the list followed by 43 in Assam, 15 in Jharkhand, 10 in Odisha, 7 each in Maharashtra and Meghalaya and 5 each in Uttar Pradesh and Manipur.[53] Many of them have been quite controversial in nature and are counter productive, encouraging contempt for law within the police. Fake encounters, staged by the police officers, resulting in the killing of even criminals are illegal and have landed senior police officers in a sea of trouble.[54]

The death of people in police action is often justified on the basis of their self-defence. Every time when police act in that way they very vaguely argue such a defence.In reality self-defence has nothing to do with most of the encounters and many of such incidents are either calculated ones or done in retaliation to the attacks against the force. Self-defence and retaliation are clearly distinguishable.The right of self-defence available to any person ends, mainly, when there is possibility to overpower the culprit without killing him. If the force does the act of killing the victim even after they get chance to overpower them it is beyond the right of self-defence. Police being a mighty force cannot always resort to the theory of self-defence especially when the opposite party is a minor group with fewer weapons. If the police fire the victim when there is chance to overpower them without killing it is retaliation. The Apex Court in **Extra Judicial Execution Victim Families Association (EEVFAM) and Ors. Vs. Union of India (UOI) and Ors**[55] has succinctly stated that the right of self-defence or private defence falls in one basket and use of excessive force or retaliatory force falls in another basket. Therefore, while a victim of aggression has a right of private defence or self-defence (recognized by Sections 96 to 106 of the Indian Penal Code) if that victim exceeds the right of private defence or self-defence by using excessive force or retaliatory measures, he then becomes an aggressor and commits a punishable offence. Unfortunately occasionally, use of excessive force or retaliation leads to the death of the original aggressor. When the State uses such excessive or retaliatory force leading to death, it is referred to as an extra-judicial killing or an extra-judicial execution.In **Darshan Singh Vs.State of Punjab and Anr.**[56], the Supreme Court has held that "when there is real apprehension that the aggressor might cause death or grievous hurt, in that event the right of private defence of the defender could even extend to causing of death. A mere reasonable apprehension is enough to put the right of self-defence into operation, but it is also settled position of law that a right of self-defence is only right to defend oneself and not to retaliate. It is not a right to take revenge.

The Rule of Law in such cases does not sanction the procedure followed. Such procedure is clearly unjust, unfair and unreasonable and, therefore, violative of the fundamental right guaranteed by Article 21 of the Constitution. For the reasons stated above, The Human Rights Commission has issued some guidelines[57] in the matter of death during the course of a police action-.

- As the information furnished to the Police officers in charge of the respective Police Stations in each of these cases is sufficient to suspect the commission of a cognizable offence, immediate steps are taken to investigate the facts and circumstances leading to the death of the PWGs, in the light of the elucidation made in this order.
- As the Police themselves in the respective cases are involved in perpetrating encounter, it would be appropriate that the cases are made over to some other investigating agency preferably the State CID. As a lot of time has already been lost, we recommend that the investigation be completed within four months from now. If the investigation results in prosecution, steps for speedy trial are to be taken. The Commission hopes that suitable compensation would be awarded in cases ending in conviction and sentence.
- Deceased Shankariah (Case No.234 (3)/93-94/NHRC) admittedly was not involved in any pending criminal case and ending his life through the process of alleged encounter was totally unjustified. So far as he is concerned, the Commission is of the view that the State Government should immediately come forward to compensate his widow by payment of compensation of Rs. 1 lakh as was done in similar cases and the police involved in killing him should be subjected to investigation and trial depending upon the outcome of investigation.
- The Commission commends to the State Police to change their practice and sensitise everyone in the State to keep the legal position in view and modulate action accordingly. In case the practice continues notwithstanding what we have now said, the quantum of compensation has to be increased in future and a stricter view of the situation has to be taken. Being aware of the fact that this practice has been in vogue for

years and the people have remained oblivious of the situation, the Commission is not contemplating the award of any interim compensation at this stage.

The Supreme Court also, on the basis of the NHRC guidelines, has issued detailed guidelines in **People's Union for Civil Liberties Vs. State of Maharashtra**[58] in the matter of killing in police actions. It is highly necessary to probe in to the fact whether the police followed these guidelines.

(b) Arbitrary Arrest and Detention

Detention is the most basic deprivation of a person's freedom. It is a limitation of a person's liberty by the exercise of police control over his movements. Human rights abuses take place in police custody despite the fact that the treatment of persons in detention is sought to be very closely regulated under both international law and domestic law. The weaker sections of society are generally the target groups in such cases. They neither have the awareness, resources and connections to save themselves. A shift in the mindset of the police and following the rules of custodial justice would go a long way in protecting the human rights of masses.[59]

The Commission has in this connection kept itself alive to the spirit of various United Nations instruments too. The International Covenant on Civil and Political Rights[60] makes it explicit that everyone has the right to liberty and security of person and nobody shall be subjected to arbitrary arrest or detention. It further mandates that anyone who has been the victim of unlawful arrest or detention shall have an enforceable right to compensation. The Convention against Torture and Other Cruel, Inhuman or Degrading Treatment or Punishment, 1985[61] makes it an obligation of the State to ensure that in its legal system, the victim of an act of torture obtains redress and has an enforceable right to fair and adequate compensation, including the means for as full a rehabilitation as possible. In the event of the death of the victim as a result of an act of torture, his dependants shall be entitled to compensation. The Body of Principles for the Protection of All Persons under Any Form of Detention or Imprisonment (1988)[62], also prescribes for remedy of compensation, in case of any damage incurred because of acts of omission by public officials contrary to the rights contained in the Body of Principles.

In the case of Sanabhai Bhulabhai Machhar[63], the Commission considered that the death occurred in suspicious circumstances and the police officials on duty did not exercise the due diligence expected of them. This case is a significant illustration of the widened scope of the meaning, which the Commission has given to the concept of immediate interim relief. The Commission took the position that it is not required in a case to establish that the public servant was negligent in preventing the violation of human rights. It is sufficient to bring the case within the doctrine of res ipsa loquitor if the concerned public servant has not exercised due diligence. The Commission has thus enhanced the meaning of Section 18(1) and has broadened the horizons of S.18(3)of the Act.

(c) **Custodial Violence/deaths**

Custodial violence is an unacceptable abuse of power and an abhorrent violation of human rights by the protectors of the law themselves. It not only violates Article 21 of the Constitution of India which guarantees the fundamental right to life and liberty, but also infringes upon Article 3 of Universal Declaration of Human Rights (UDHR) and Article 6 of the International Covenant on Civil and Political Rights, that every person has the right to life, liberty and security and no one shall be arbitrarily deprived of life. The Commission has played an active role in redressing the grievances of the victims of custodial violence. In accordance with a circular dated 14 December 1993 issued by the Commission to all State authorities, all cases of custodial deaths either in police or in judicial custody are required to be brought to the notice of the Commission within twenty-four hours. The illustrative cases on custodial death reveal that the interventions of the Commission are increasingly securing better investigation of such cases and resulting in the provision of immediate interim relief to the survivors of the deceased victims of custodial violence. In this connection, the Commission would like to recall the Judgement of the Supreme Court in the case of **D.K. Basu Vs State of West Bengal**[64], which dealt with the principle Ubi jus, ibl remedium i.e., there is no wrong without a remedy. The law wills that in every case where a man is wronged and damaged, he must have a remedy. A mere declaration of the invalidity of an action, or the finding of custodial violence or death in a lock-up, does not by itself provide any meaningful remedy to a person whose fundamental right to life has been infringed. Much more needs to be done. While there is no express provision in the Constitution of India for grant of compensation for violation of the fundamental right to life, the Supreme Court has judicially evolved a right to compensation in cases of established unconstitutional deprivation of person's right to liberty or life.

The National Human Rights Commission soon after its constitution in October,1993, called upon the law and order agencies at the district level throughout the country to report matters relating to custodial death and custodial rape within 24 hours of occurrence. Since then ordinarily reports of such incidents have been coming to the Commission through the official district agencies. The Commission is deeply disturbed over the rising incidents of death in police lock-up and jails. Scrutiny of the reports in respect of all these custodial deaths by the Commission very often shows that the post-mortem in many cases has not been done properly. Usually the reports are drawn up casually and do not at all help in the forming of an opinion as to the cause of death. The Commission has formed an impression that a systematic attempt is being made to suppress the truth and the report is merely the police version of the incident. The post-mortem report was intended to be the most valuable record and considerable importance was being placed on this document in drawing conclusions about the death. The Commission is of a prima-facie view that the local doctor succumbs to police pressure which leads to distortion of the facts. The Commission made it mandatory that all post- mortem examinations done in respect of deaths in police custody and in jails should be video-filmed and cassettes be sent to the Commission along with the post-mortem report. While doing so, the Commission was alive to the fact that the process of video-filming will involve extra cost but the Commission considered human life to be more valuable than the cost of video-filming as such occasions should be very limited and introduced video-filming of post mortem exami-nation with effect from 1st October, 1995.

However, the analysis of latest data clearly indicates that custodial violence and deaths cases are still deeply existing in out system. Uttar Pradesh has registered highest number of cases of custodial deaths in the country between October 2015 and September this year, with as many as 401 deaths taking place in judicial custody and 27 in policy custody. During the period (October 2015 and September 2016), maximum 32,498 complaints were registered against police, out of which 206 cases were of encounter. "Chhattisgarh with 66 encounter cases, topped the list followed by 43 in Assam, 15 in Jharkhand, 10 in Odisha, 7 each in Maharashtra and Meghalaya, 5 each in Uttar Pradesh and Manipur. West Bengal with 11 cases, topped the list of registered cases of encounter by Para-Military forces. Between October, 2015 and September, 2016, the NHRC has registered 1,05,664 cases on the basis of complaints, intimation from police and prison authorities etc. and on suo motu basis. The number of cases registered during the period on suo motu basis is 133. During the corresponding period in 2014-15 and 2013-14, it registered 1,17,477 and 1,06,684 cases respectively. The public authorities complying with the Commissions recommendations paid Rs 11,59,56,172 as monetary relief in 410 cases to the victims or their kin. These included cases of the previous year as well as the some cases wherein recommendations were made during 2015-2016. [65]

From 2001 to 2010, the national Human Rights Commission (nHRC) recorded 14,231 i.e. 4.33 persons died in police and judicial custody in india. This includes 1,504 deaths in police custody and 12,727 deaths in judicial custody from 2001-2002 to 2009-2010.1 A large majority of these deaths are a direct consequence of torture in custody. These deaths reflect only a fraction of the problem with torture and custodial deaths in india. not all the cases of deaths in police and prison custody are reported to the nHRC. The nHRC does not have jurisdiction over the armed forces under section 19 of the Human Rights Protection Act. Further, the nHRC does not record statistics of torture not resulting into death. Torture remains endemic, institutionalised and central to the administration of justice and counter-terrorism measures. india has demonstrated no political will to end torture.

The NHRC recorded 1504 deaths in police custody during 2001-2010 which includes 165 deaths in 2001-2002;2 183 deaths in 2002-2003;3162 deaths in 2003-2004;4136 deaths in 2004-2005;5139 deaths in 2005-2006;6119 deaths in 2006-2007; 7187 deaths in 2007-2008;8142 deaths in 2008-2009; 124 deaths in 2009-2010 and 147 deaths in 2010-2011.9 The Asian Centre for Human Rights (ACHR) has consistently underlined that about 99.99% of deaths in police custody can be ascribed to torture and occur within 48 hours of the victims being taken into custody.

The NHRC also recorded 12,727 deaths in judicial custody from 2001-2002 to 2009-10. These included 1,140 cases in 2001-2002;[66]1,157 cases in 2002-2003;[67]1,300 cases in 2003-2004;[68] 1,357 cases in 2004-2005;[69] 1,591 cases in 2005-2006;[70]1,477 cases in 2006-2007;[71]1,789 cases in 2007-2008;[72]1,532 cases in 2008-2009;[73] 1,389 cases in 2009-2010 upto 28 February 2010. in other words, an average of 1,416 persons died year during this period. A large number of such deaths in judicial custody take place as a result of torture, denial of medical facilities and inhuman prison conditions that amount to torture, inhuman or degrading treatment.

Further, the data of the NHRC does not reflect the actual extent of custodial death in india. As stated above not all custodial deaths are reported to the NHRC. For example, the Asian Centre for Human Rights filed a complaint with regard to the custodial death of Jumchi nguso (35 years) as a result of torture at the naharlagun police station in Papumpare district of Arunachal Pradesh on 15 July 2010[74]. The NHRC registered the case and closed it after the State government awarded compensation of Rs 5 lakhs. Yet the NHRC's official statistics for 2010-2011 show that there was no custodial death during the year in Arunachal Pradesh. Similarly, ACHR filed two complaints of custodial deaths from Meghalaya i.e. death of Dilip Dohkrud (35 years) due to alleged torture at the Bholaganj Police Check Post under shella Police station in East Khasi Hills district on 27 January 2010. The data of the NHRC does not reflect the actual extent of custodial death in india. As stated above not all custodial deaths are reported to the NHRC. For example, the Asian Centre for Human Rights filed a complaint with regard to the custodial death of Jumchi nguso (35 years) as a result of torture at the naharlagun police station in Papumpare district of Arunachal Pradesh on 15 July 2010[75]. The NHRC registered the case and closed it after the State government awarded compensation of Rs 5 lakhs. Yet the NHRC's official statistics for 2010-2011 show that there was no custodial death during the year in Arunachal Pradesh. Similarly, ACHR filed two complaints of custodial deaths from Meghalaya i.e. death of Dilip Dohkrud (35 years) due to alleged torture at the Bholaganj Police Check Post under shella Police station in East Khasi Hills district on 27 January 2010[76] and the death of Dexstarwise Bamon (28 years) at the Ladrymbai Police lock-up in

Jowai on 26 January 2010[77]. However, the official statistics record only one death during April 2009 to March 2010.

(d) Gujarat Riots

The Commission dealt in some detail with the human rights situation in Gujarat, beginning with the tragedy that occurred in Godhra on 27 February 2002 when the Sabarmati Express was attacked and set on fire, and the large-scale communal violence that subsequently ensued. The NHRC noted that numerous allegations had been made that FIRs were being distorted or poorly recorded and that senior political personalities sought to influence investigations by remaining present in police stations. In particullar, The NHRC expressed concern about the widespread lack of faith in the integrity of the investigating process and the ability of those conducting investigations. The Commission directed the Gujarat government that in particular the incidents at Godhra, Gulmarg Society, Naroda Patia, Sardarpura and Best Bakery in Vadodara be entrusted to the CBI so that the integrity of the process could be restored. The commission also recommended that Special Courts be created to try these critical cases and that Special Cells be constituted with District Magistrates monitoring the progress of the investigation of cases not handled by the CBI. The NHRC further recommended that senior political leaders and officers visit the camps in order to restore the confidence of victimsand that displaced person should not be asked to leave camps until appropriate relief and safety measures are in place Recognizing the dire needs of hundreds of destitute women, orphans and those subjected to rape in distress, the NHRC's recommendations call on government agencies to ensure that they receive proper counseling and psychological care.

The Commission also observed that the right to fair trial is a Constitutional imperative and fairness of a trial includes, proper protection of the rights of the accused as also the capacity of witnesses to come forth to make true and faithful statements in respect of matters within their knowledge, without any fear or favour and further that fair trial envisages a fair deal to the victims also. The Commission, therefore, asked the Director General of Police, Gujarat to respond to the following query:"Whether any measures have been taken to protect the safety, physical and psychological well-being, dignity and privacy of victims and witnesses who have to depose either in court or before the Commission of Enquiry and, if so, the nature of that protection to enable them to depose freely and fearlessly."

Deeply concerned about the damage to the credibility of the criminal justice delivery system and negation of human rights of victims, the National Human Rights Commission, on consideration of the report of its team which was sent to Vadodara, has filed a Special Leave Petition[78] in the Supreme Court with a prayer to set aside the impugned judgment of the Trial Court in the Best Bakery case and sought directions for further investigation by an independent agency and retrial of the case in a competent court located outside the State of Gujarat. Responding to the query as to what measures have been taken to protect the safety, physical and psychological well being of the victims and witnesses, the DGP has indicated that in the absence of any specific complaint from any witness/victim, it would not be possible for the State Police to accord protection to each and every witness/victim. He has stated that witnesses are free to approach the police officers seeking protection. The DGP has then assured this Commission that all the Superintendents of Police and Commissioners of Police have been duly instructed to ensure that due protection is given immediately whenever any witness/victim requests for the same or expresses apprehension to his safety.

The Commission observed that the State has failed to discharge its primary and inescapable resp onsibility to protect the rights to life, liberty, equality and dignity of all of those who constitute it. The principle of res ipsa loquitur (the affair speaking for itself) applies in this case in assessing the degree of State responsibility in the failure to protect the Constitutional rights of the people of Gujarat. The responsibility of the

State extended not only to the acts of its own agents, but also to those of non-State players within its jurisdiction and to any action that may cause or facilitate the violation of human rights.

(e) Harassment of Undertrials

The Commission received a complaint from Mohammed Nizam and Mohammed Hashim stating that they had been falsely implicated in a case allegedly of the murder of one Devki Kumari. They stated that Devki Kumari had, in fact appeared in court and given a statement under section 164 Criminal Procedure Code (Cr.PC.) indicating that she was alive. The complainants had, however, been sent to jail and denied bail. In response to the Commission's notice, a report was received from the Superintendent of Police, Madhepura, Bihar which stated that a case under section 302 Indian Penal Code (IPC) was pending against the complainants. The Commission, however, received and considered a further representation by the complainants, enclosing an acquittal order of the court, which also directed the State Government to initiate action against the errant police officers. The Commission reached the conclusion that this was a case in which the complainants had been humiliated in the eyes of the public and unnecessarily dragged before a Court under the serious charge of murder because of faulty investigation reports by the police. The Commission accordingly awarded compensation of Rs. 20,000 to each of the complainants as immediate interim relief and also directed the recovery of this amount from the police officers who were guilty of the faulty investigation.

However, inspite of large efforts by the Commission, the fact remains is that India may not have enough safeguards to protect its citizens from human rights violations by the police when we take into count and analyze the official data. From 2012 to 2015, cases with the NHRC against the police have always been more than 30,000, constituting around 30 per cent of all the cases it receives. As many as 35,831 cases were registered against the police with the National Human Rights Commission (NHRC) in 2015-16 and only 94 first information reports were registered in 2015 on the other hand.[79], alarmingly big gap which clearly shows that there is unwillingness among the police to file an FIR against one of their own. In the absence of a body similar to the Independent Police Complaints Commission as in the United Kingdom or the Independent Police Investigative Directorate in South Africa, allegations of human rights violations by the police in India are investigated by the police themselves. The NHRC's investigative unit draws its members from the State police forces who are on deputation. The unit does not have the powers for active investigation: that is to say, it cannot collect or preserve physical evidence itself but has to ask the local police for it. Wherever an offence has been made out after an inquiry, the NHRC, depending on the nature of the case, recommends lawful action, which may include punitive measures against the guilty and monetary relief to the victim. . However, question to be asked is that whether there is any follow-up after the NHRC recommends monetary relief? Handing out money, though vital for many complainants who have medical bills to pay, does not mean that justice has been served. In fact, from April 2012 to July 2015, the NHRC recommended disciplinary action in just 22 cases and prosecution for a lone policeman, though monetary relief was recommended in 450 cases from April 2013 to March 2015. Further, in seven of the 10 years from 2006 to 2015, not a single policeman was convicted of human rights violations.

CHAPTER -III
ECONOMIC SOCIAL AND CULTURAL RIGHTS

- **BACKGROUND**

The Universal Declaration of Human Rights adopted by the General Assembly on 10th December, 1948, was followed by two Covenants namely the International Covenant on Civil and Political Rights (ICCPR), 1966 and International Covenant on Economic, Social and Cultural Rights (ICESCR), 1966. India signed both these International Conventions in 1979. In democratic societies, fundamental human rights are broadly classified into civil and political rights on the one hand and economic, social and cultural rights on the other.

The object of both sets of rights is to make an individual an effective participant in the affairs of the society. Unless both sets of rights are available, neither full development of the human personality can be achieved nor can it be said that true democracy exists. Unfortunately, however, protection of economic, social and cultural rights compared to the protection of civil and political rights, both at the national and international level, has been poor and irregular.

- **INTERNATIONAL EFFORTS**

The UN Committee on Economic, Social and Cultural Rights (CESCR) is taking a robust attitude towards practical implementation of economic, social and cultural rights. It was recognised by the UN in 1986 when it acknowledged the Right to Development as a human right. The right to development as formulated in the 1986 UN Declaration is a synthesis of the two sets of rights. The distinction, long made, between civil and political rights on the one hand and the economic, social and cultural rights on the other was put to rest by the Vienna Declaration and Programme of Action, which affirms that all human rights are universal, indivisible and inter-independent and inter-related". The Declaration, however, will amount to a little more than an aspiration till the economic, social and cultural rights are in reality made available to the vast sections of the population. The National Human Rights Institutions have a great role to play to correct the fallacy of treating one set of rights as inferior to the other set of rights so that they can implement economic, social and cultural rights in the political and social contexts in which they operate.

- **CONSTITUTIONAL AMENDMENTS**

The Indian Constitution was amended by the Eighty Sixth Constitutional Amendment Act 2002 and it now proclaims[80] that the State shall provide free and compulsory education to all children of the age of six to fourteen years in such manner as the State may, by law, determine." Further, the rights of a person, arrested and detained by the State authorities, are also provided in Indian Constitution[81]. These also includes the, right to be informed of the grounds of arrest and the right to legal advice and the right to be produced before a magistrate within 24 hours of arrest[82]. The Constitution also gurantees right against exploitation which includes prohibition of trafficking in human beings and forced labour and prohibition of employment of children below 14 years of age to work in any factory or mine or in any other hazardous employment.[83] Further, subject to public order and morality, all persons are equally entitled to freedom of conscience and the right to profess, practise and propagate religion[84]. And every religious denomination or section also has the right to establish and maintain religious institutions and manage their religious affairs[85]. Under the Indian Constitution, no one can be compelled to pay any religious taxes[86] and the wholly State-funded educational institutions are barred from imparting religious instructions[87]. The rights of any section of citizens or a minority to promote its distinct language, script or culture, to have access to State-funded educational institutions[88], and to establish and maintain educational institutions of its choice[89] are also guaranteed.

- **THE CLASSIFICATION ERROR**

The right to Constitutional remedies is essentially the right to move the Supreme Court of India for enforcement of the above rights[90]. The Supreme Court is vested with wide Constitutional powers in this regard and it include the power to issue directions, orders or writs for the enforcement of the fundamental rights[91]. State (i.e. provincial) High Courts too have identical powers.[92]. As laws inconsistent with or in derogation of the rights conferred by part Ill of the Constitution are void[93], the Courts have the power to adjudge the Constitutional validity of all laws. Furthermore, the law declared by the Supreme Court shall be binding on all courts in India.[94]

Judicially non-enforceable rights under the Constitution[95] are chiefly those of economic and social in character. However, The Constitution[96] makes it clear, their judicial non-enforceability does not weaken the duty of State to apply them in making laws, since they are "Nevertheless fundamental in the governance of the country" Additionally, the innovative jurisprudence of the Supreme Court has not read into Article 21(The right of life and personal liberty) many of these principles and made them enforceable.[97] The duties of the State encompass security of a social order with justice, social, economic and political, striving to minimize and eliminate all inequalities [98], Security for "The citizens, men and women equally" and the right to an adequate means of livelihood[99] Distribution of ownership and control of community resources to sub serve the common good[100], prevention of concentration of wealth and means of production of the common detriment ([101] Securing of equal pay for equal work for both men and women[102] preventing of abuse of labour, including child labour[103] Ensuring of child development[104] Ensuring of equal Justice and free legal aid[105], Organization of village democracies[106] Provisions of the right work education and public assistance in case of unemployment, old age sickness and disability[107], Provision of humane conditions of work[108] living wage and a decent standard of life[109], Securing of participation of workers in the management of industries[110] provisions of uniform civil code for the whole country[111] Provision of free and compulsory education for all children under fourteen years[112], Promotion of educational and economic interests of weaker sections of the people and their protection from injustice and all forms of exploitation [113] Raising of the standard of living, improving the level of nutrition and public health and prohibition or intoxication drinks and of drugs[114], Scientific reorganization of animal husbandry-and agricultural economy[115] protection of monuments and things of artistic or historical importance[116] Separation of judiciary from executive[117] and Promotion of international peace and Security[118].

- **ESCR under the UDHR and the Constitution**

The table below shows that most of the economic, social and cultural rights proclaimed in the Universal Declaration of Human Rights have been incorporated in part IV of the Indian Constitution-

No.	Name of the Economic, Social or Cultural Right	The Universal Declaration of Human Rights	Part IV of The Constitution of India
1	Right to work, to just and favourable conditions of work	Article 23(1)	Article 41
2	Right to equal pay for equal work	Article 23(2)	Article 39(d)
3	Right to education	Article 26(1)	Articles 21-A, 41, 45 & 51A(k)
4	Right to just and favourable remuneration	Article 23(3)	Article 43
5	Right to rest and Leisure	Article 24	Article 43
6	Right of everyone to a standard of living adequate for him and his family	Article 25(1)	Article 39(a) & Article 47
7	Right to a proper social order	Article 28	Article 38

THE INDIAN CONSTITUTION lays great emphasis on-both categories of rights and two important chapters, that is, Fundamental Rights and Directive Principles of State Policy are devoted to them. The fundamental rights mainly deal with civil and political rights while the Directive Principles of State Policy elaborately deal with economic, social and cultural rights. Though the Directive Principles said to be non-justiciable and unenforceable as per Article 37 of the Constitution, but, the recent trend of creative judicial interpretation makes them enforceable for all practical purposes. Furthermore the principles therein laid down are nevertheless fundamental in the governance of the country and it shall be the duty of the State to apply these principles in making laws.

In India, the Courts have been reading Civil and Political Rights into the Economic, Social and Cultural Rights by construing the two sets of rights harmoniously – by expanding the concept of "right to life and liberty" to mean the right to live with human dignity and all that goes with it. The Courts in India have related health care, food security and elementary education with "Right to Life" and thereby ensured their "enforceability". It is also the firm view of the Indian Commission, that we must accept indivisibility and inter-related-nature of the two sets of rights for full development of human personality. To effectively implement economic, social and cultural rights, we need to adopt a rights based approach. While Legislative policy, Judicial directions and Executive action are the three main requirements of the conceptualization of social, economic and cultural rights, there is a sacred duty vested with the State in the realization of these rights. There should be no doubt, dispute or ambiguity on this account.

While stuck with its role for better protection of human rights, the Commission has been intervening, from time to time, in the matters concerning human rights in the proceedings pending in the Supreme Court or the High Courts in India with a view to put forth its point of view before the court and also to assist the court for consideration. A brief mention may be made of some of the important remittances received from the Supreme Court / High Courts or interventions made by the Commission in some important areas concerning human rights before the aforesaid courts.

(a) Orissa Starvation Case[119]

The Indian Council of Legal Aid and Advice and others had filed a Writ Petition (civil) No. 42/97 before the Supreme Court of India inviting attention to starvation deaths in the KBK Districts of Orissa despite the direction of the Apex court in an earlier case reported as 1989 Supp. (1) SCC 258. On the basis of information furnished by the petitioner before the Supreme Court about an intervention of the Commission on a complaint, the Supreme Court vide its order dated 28/4/97 and 26/7/97 directed the petitioner to submit suggestions before the Commission for further consideration of the matter. While dealing with the matter the Commission observed that the expression "right to life" contained in Article 21 of the Constitution has been judicially interpreted as not merely life of survival or animal existence but a "life with human dignity". It follows therefore, that the State is obliged to provide at least those minimum requirements which are essential to enable a person to live with human dignity and right to food is inherent to live with dignity. As a result of the intervention by the Commission, the Government of Orissa proposed short term and long-term measures of development to end the scourge of deprivation, malnutrition and cyclical starvation in the KBK Districts of Orissa. As a part of monitoring of the situation in the three Districts on a continuing basis, the Commission sought and examined quarterly performance appraisal reports relating to the achievement of physical and financial targets. The Commission took assistance of its Special Rapporteur for keeping it fully informed of the various developments in the three districts and also to interact on its behalf with the concerned authorities at the State, District and other levels. The key areas of concern for the Commission included rural water supply and sanitation, primary health care, social security schemes, soil conservation, rural development, afforestation, land reforms, SC/ST development and school education.

The Commission considered the reports submitted by the Special Rapporteur which presented a satisfactory picture about the execution of long-term action plan under the various heads. The Commission considered the crucial role of the revised longterm action plan proposed, in achieving the ultimate objective of drought proofing, poverty alleviation and development saturation to improving the quality of life of the people in KBK districts and recommended to the Planning Commission for further extension of RLTAP beyond March 2007. It also recommended execution of all projects under a system of surveillance and monitoring and hope for encouraging action both by the State Government as well as by the Government of India. In order to deal with the scourge of starvation, the Commission considered short term and long term measures in key areas of health, employment, poverty alleviation, drinking water supply etc. in the State of Orissa and their implementation is being monitored by the Commission.

(b) Custodial Disappearances Case[120]

The Hon'ble Supreme Court of India vide its order dated 31/1/2003 referred the subject matter of investigation in Special Leave to Appeal (Civil) No. 7436/99 arising from the judgement and order dated 24/12/98 of the High Court of Guwahati filed by Ms. Romila Hazarika against Union of India and others for tracing out of her missing brother Dambarudhar Hazarika after his alleged release from custody by army personnel. The court directed that the matter may be referred to the Commission for further investigation. Accordingly, the Commission directed spot investigation by a team of its officers. However, despite best efforts by the team, the whereabouts of Dambarudhar Hazarika could not be traced and he continued to be missing. The Commission informed the Apex Court accordingly.

(c) Punjab Mass Cremation Case[121]

The Commission received a remit, from the Supreme Court of India to examine 2007 cremations of dead bodies as un-identified by the Punjab Police in the Police District of Amritsar, Majitha and Tarn Taran, Punjab during the period w.e.f. 1984 to 1994. The Hon'ble Supreme Court of India also separately directed the CBI to take further action into the matter and register the cases where necessary, hold investigations and proceed in accordance with the law on the basis of material collected through investigation. In furtherance of the remit, the Commission considered the matter from time to time and it has unhesitantly held till now that human rights of 194 persons, who were admittedly in the custody of the police immediately prior to their death, stood invaded and infringed when they lost their lives, while in custody of the police thereby rendering the state vicariously liable. There was a very great responsibility on the part of the police and other authorities to take reasonable care so that citizens in their custody were 'safe and not deprived of their right to life as in such cases the duty of care on the part of the State is strict and admits of non-exception."

The State of Punjab was, therefore, held accountable and vicariously responsible for the infringement of the indefeasible right to life of those 194 deceased persons as it failed to "safeguard their lives and persons against the risk of avoidable harm."

The Commission has awarded a total compensation of Rs.4,85,00,000/- @ Rs. 2.50 lakhs to the next of kin of each of 194 deceased persons who were admittedly in the custody of the Punjab Police at the time of their death. The Commission is in the process of examining the remaining claims.

(d) Commission not to sit as an Appellate Body[122]

The Hon'ble Supreme Court of Ind a vide its order dated 28/1/2004 referred a matter relating to Special Leave to Appeal (Civil) No. 34/2003 (State of J&K Vs. Kamal Goria and others). In the said SLP, the order passed by the Hon'ble J&K High Court on 6/9/2002 extending all migrants from militancy affected areas the same benefits as have been given to the migrants from Kashmir Valley was challenged by the State of J&K before the Apex Court. The Commission while considering the matter on 10/8/2004 observed that it could not sit in appeal over the jugement and order of the High Court and it is only the Supreme Court which has jurisdiction to decide the appeal. Accordingly, the reference was returned to the Hon'ble Supreme Court to decide the SLP on the judicial side.

(e) **Relief to Mentally ill in Prisons**[123]

The Commission received an intimation from the office of DG (Prisons), Delhi about languishing in jail since 28/10/85 of a mentally ill prisoner Charanjit who was accused in a murder case bearing FIR No. 854/85 registered at P.S. Adarsh Nagar. Deeply concerned about the need to protect the human rights of the under-trial prisoner, the Commission, filed an application before the Delhi High Court under section 482 Cr.P.C. seeking the quashing of the trial in view of the inordinate delay in the case. The High Court allowed the intervention application. As a result of the initiative taken by the Commission, offers were made by the VIMHANS for extending medical facilities and treatment free of cost and by the Help Age India to take over the patient and accommodate him in their half way home or old-age home after the VIMHANS certified that the condition of the patient was stable. Accordingly, orders for shifting of the patient to VIMHANS were pronounced by the High Court on 31st July, 2003. Subsequently, the Commission moved a Criminal Writ Petition No. 1278/04 before the High Court of Delhi and prayed for quashing of the trial of Charanjeet Singh whose condition had deteriorated despite prolong treatment at various hospitals/ institutions. The High Court vide its order dated 4/3/2005 quashed the trial of the mentally ill prisoner. The High Court commended the initiative and the promise by the Govt, of NCT of Delhi for taking care of medical need of Charanjit Singh after quashing of the trial. Guidelines proposed by the NHRC for considering the cases of such mentally ill under-trial was accepted by the court and suitable direction issued to the Govt, of Delhi in this regard. [Case No. 3628/30/2001-2002] During his visit to Central Jail, Ambala on 18;n October 2003, the case of a mentally ill prisoner Jai Singh came to the notice of the Chairperson, NHRC. It appeared that, after his admission to jail in case FIR No. 28 dated 3.3.76 u/s 302/ 34 IPC, he was transferred to

Mental Hospital, Amritsar on 9/5/79 for treatment. He had not been able to stand the trial, presumably because of his mental condition. He was never produced in the trial court for trial in the said case and continued as an under-trial prisoner for over 26 years.

The NHRC, in order to achieve the object of protecting and promoting human rights and to prevent further violation of human rights of life and liberty of the under trial prisoner Jai Singh, approached the Hon"ble High Court of Punjab & Haryana for appropriate orders/directions in the interest of justice. Subsequently, the Commission came to know that the case of under trial prisoner Jai Singh is already being considered along with similar other persons by the Hon'ble High Court in CWP 10791/2002. However, the intervention application filed on behalf of the Commission on 23/8/2004 was allowed by the Hon'ble Punjab and Haryana High Court. The Hon'ble High Court approved and adopted the guidelines framed by the Delhi High Court in the case of Shri Charanjeet Singh and quashed the case against Shri Jai Singh. The Court dealt with the cases of 13 mentally challenged prisoners and passed appropriate orders in each case. The Court expressed a hope that governments of UT Chandigarh and the States of Punjab and Haryana will keep in mind the guidelines while dealing with the cases of menially challenged prisoners.

(f) Monitoring of the functioning of three mental hospitals in Ranchi. Agra and Gwalior

The Commission commenced to oversee the functioning of the Ranchi Institute of Neuro- Psychiatry and Allied Sciences (RINPAS), Ranchi, the Institute of Mental Health and Hospital (IMHH), Agra and Gwalior Mansik Arogyashala, (GMA), Gwalior, under the Supreme Court order dated 11.11.97. The Commission has been monitoring the performance of these institutions in regard to clearly specified tasks given by the Supreme Court while granting autonomy to these institutions. RINPAS is making steady strides towards realization of the objectives set by the Supreme Court by improving the diagnostic and therapeutic facilities, developing the social and occupational rehabilitation facilities and expanding the community services and research activities. RINPAS is running regular M.Phil and Ph.D courses in clinical psychology and psychiatric social work with affiliation to Ranchi University. RINPAS has also been selected as a Nodal point for District Mental Health at Dhumka (Jharkhand). The Commission has been evaluating the performance of these three mental institutes every year in relation to the task assigned by the Hon'ble Supreme Court of India and submitting regular reports before the Supreme Court.

Thus, it can be seen that the NHRC of India enjoys a unique position within the framework of the State structure in terms of its role as protector and promoter of human rights. Its true responsibility is thus not to be seen as a replacement of or alternative to an independent and impartial judiciary that enforces its rulings. The NHRC and the judiciary perform separate and independent functions. The judiciary determines the legal obligations with respect to the human rights law. It interprets the constitutionality of human rights, evolves the jurisprudence and ensures respect for law. The judiciary is designed with an enforcement mechanism. The ruling given by the Supreme Court is binding on all courts in the country. The Supreme Court is empowered to give directions to public authorities. In a remit, the Supreme Court assigned specific cases of human rights violations for monitoring, to NHRC. These included the bonded labour situation in the country, the management of the mental health hospitals at Agra, Gwalior and Ranchi, the Agra Protective Home, the prevalence of silicosis in the country and the issues regarding the right to food in the context of starvation deaths in Odhisha. These cases are monitored through the Special Rapporteurs of NHRC who make field visits to the states, meet the officials of the concerned state governments, propose action and submit reports to the Commission which after due deliberation and approval are submitted to the Supreme Court for further directions. As clarified by the Apex Court[124], in cases referred to it by the Supreme

Court, the NHRC acts as an extended arm of the Supreme Court and the jurisdiction exercised by the NHRC in these cases is of a special nature and is not affected by any limitation of the PHR Act. Though the judiciary has relaxed the rules of standing in matters of public interest it is not easy for the citizens at the grassroots level to approach the High Court or the Supreme Court. As compared to the courts, the victims of human rights violations have greater physical access to the NHRC. It can take cognisance of any human right violation suo motu or on the basis of a petition before it. Having taken cognisance of a human rights violation, the NHRC can itself investigate and make recommendations to the authorities concerned or it can approach the Courts. The NHRC has an advantage over the judiciary in so far as its powers of taking suo-motu cognisance of a human rights violation are concerned. A court on the other hand can act only when it is approached. The NHRC, as per practice does not entertain petitions which relate to violation of human rights if these are pending in courts and dismisses such petitions in limini. In such matters the NHRC on merits, can seek the permission of the court to intervene in the proceedings. The NHRC can assist the victims in airing contentious issues before the court and provide legal services. It can become the voice of the suffering and helpless people by supporting their cases. NHRC's support will give a greater legitimacy to the human rights victims and assist them in securing justice.

The hon'ble Supreme Court in **Paramjit Kaur vs. State of Punjab**[125] clarified that in cases referred to the NHRC by the Supreme Court, the Commission was acting sui generic and as an extended arm of the Supreme Court, not fettered by any limitation of the PHR Act. The Supreme Court observed that the NHRC headed by a former Chief Justice of India is a unique expert body in itself. The Chairman of the Commission, in his capacity as a Judge of the Supreme Court and also as Chief Justice of India and so also two of its other members who have held high judicial offices as Chief Justices of the High Courts, and have throughout their tenure expounded and enforced fundamental rights are in their own way, experts in the field. In deciding matters referred by the Supreme Court, NHRC is given a free hand and is not circumscribed by any conditions. Therefore, the jurisdiction exercised by the NHRC in these matters is of a special nature not covered by enactment or law.

Hence, it can be seen that the Commission has a symbiotic relationship with the Supreme Court. The cases remitted by the Supreme Court to the NHRC are vigorously monitored by the Commission. On the directions of the Supreme Court the NHRC is monitoring the bonded labour and child labour situation in the country. It has also been assigned the responsibility of monitoring three mental hospitals and a protective home. According to Justice Verma, the former Chairperson of NHRC, the close working relationship between the NHRC and the Supreme Court is an illustration of the strategic alliance between the two institutions to secure the rights of the vulnerable.

CHAPTER -IV
RIGHTS OF WOMEN

The principle of gender equality is enshrined in the Indian Constitution in its Preamble, Fundamental Rights, Directive Principles and Fundamental Duties. In accordance with the spirit of the Article 14 and 15 of the Constitution of India, which provide for equality before law and non-discrimination respectively, India has ratified the CEDAW. Under international law, India has the obligation to act with due diligence to prevent, investigate and punish the acts of violence by both the state and non state actors and provide compensation to victims.[126] The Constitution not only grants equality to women, but also empowers the State to adopt measures of positive discrimination in favour of women. Within the framework of a democratic polity, the development policies, laws, plans and programmes have aimed at women's advancements in different spheres. The 73rd and 74th Amendments to the Constitution of India in the year 1993 provided for reservations of seats in the local bodies of Panchayats and Municipalities for women, thus laying a strong foundation for their participation in decision-making at the local levels. India has also ratified various international conventions and human rights instruments for securing equal rights of women. Key among them is the ratification of the Convention on the Elimination of All Forms of Discrimination Against Women (CEDAW) in 1993. Ever since the Commission came into existence on the 12th of October 1993, its efforts to protect and promote the rights of women have evolved in a variety of interconnected ways. India being a signatory to CEDAW and its First Country Report was due to be submitted to the Committee established under the treaty in 1994, the Commission initially recommended vigorous implementation of the country's obligations under this Convention. A Member of the Commission participated in the Fourth United Nations Conference on Women that was held in Beijing in September 1995. The Commission recommended that well-coordinated steps be taken to act upon the Declaration and Programme of Action adopted at that Conference and also to oversee the implementation of the commitments of India under the CEDAW, a matter on which the Commission attaches the highest importance. A large number of legislations are also in place seeking to protect and safeguard rights of women and promote their status in the society. However, proper implementation of these legislations as well as policies and programmes have been a problem area. Hence, a large percentage of women in India still suffer from various disadvantages and denial of their legitimate rights.

1. Right to Health

It next considered the violation of the rights of women from the angle of health. The issue of maternal anaemia was first identified as a human rights issue in the year 1996-97. Following a communication received from a leading medical authority, the Commission took serious note of the wide prevalence of iron and iodine deficiency related health problems in expectant mothers and their newly born children, who either died during delivery or were born with mental disabilities. In the view of the Commission, insensitivity to such a situation amounted to a callous disregard to right to life with dignity and reasonable health. The Commission thus undertook a review of the steps that were being taken at the Central and State levels to deal with this problem. In the course of its efforts, the Commission worked closely with the concerned Ministries and Departments of the Government of India, UNICEF and other experts.

This effort of the Commission continued in the ensuing years and in the year 2000, it organised a Workshop on Health and Human

Rights in India with Special Reference to Maternal Anaemia in collaboration with the Department of Women and Child Development and UNICEF. This Workshop made some valuable recommendations. Prominent among them are - 'right to health' be declared as a Fundamental Right; education of all children be made a fundamental right and NHRC should continue to interact with government agencies, NGOs and the civil society at large through periodic consultations and reviews to end all types of discrimination against women and girl children. The detailed recommendations of the Workshop were sent to the concerned Ministries/Departments for follow-up action. Due to Commission's persistent efforts, some of these recommendations have been implemented in practice, for example, compulsory education of all children between the ages of 6 and 14 years has now become a Fundamental Right. Similarly, the courts in India have related health care with 'right to life' by expanding Article 21 of the Constitution. In the year 2000 and later in 2001, a Workshop on Human Rights and HIV/AIDS and a Consultation on Public Health and Human Rights were also organised, both of which had direct relevance to the rights of women.

2. Supervision over Protective/Custodial Homes

While the Commission was focussing its attention on the health rights of women, the Supreme Court of India, through an order dated 11 November 1997, requested the Commission to involve itself in the supervision of the Agra Protective Home in order to "ensure that the Home functions in the manner as is expected for achieving the object for which it has been set up". With a view to suggesting an appropriate course of action, a Member of the Commission along with the Member Secretary of the National Commission for Women and the Executive Director of the Central Social Welfare Board paid a visit to the Agra Protective Home in the year 1997 itself and submitted a report to the Commission. Ever since Commission's intervention in the matter, there has been substantial improvement in many areas of functioning of this institution.

Most often, in cases of sexual assault, many a times, the victims are discouraged by the community and even by the police for recorting to legal remedy. Such an example came in light when the NHRC took suo motu cognizance on a news aired by the news channel Aaj Tak on 28 may 2009 wherein it was alleged that a woman prisoner who was in judicial custody in Tihar Jail had become pregnant.[127] The commission called for a report the Inspector General of Prisons, Delhi in which it was informed that on the request of the female prisoner, the pregnancy was medically terminated at D.D.U. Hospital of Delhi on 26 may 2009. Further, fearing the stigma and other repercussions, the victim refused to divulge the details of the incident to the jail authorities. The commission after considering the report, observed that although the victim did not make any complaint against any person or official of the jail and also refused to divulge the name of the person but it was clear that she became pregnant while in judicial custody and it clearly showed a lapse on the part of the jail administration. The NHRC investigation team conducted a spot inquiry of the victim in camera but failed to collect any evidence to establish the identity of the person guilty of sexual exploitation of the victim but the team reported serious lapse in the security arrangements in the jail. The commission directed the Tihar Jail administration to immediately take steps to ensure complete security of the female prisoners in particular and to submit detailed report of the steps taken. The jail administration after taking appropriate steps submitted report to the NHRC and the Commission is further reviewing it.

3. Gender based Violence/Discrimination

While the Criminal Justice System in India has proved to be unable to respond to the needs of widespread gender based violence and atrocities against women, the NHRC is working hard to point out for greater accountability from the police and jail authorities, who are seen

PROTECTION OF HUMAN RIGHTS 75

to be insensitive to such cases due to traditional and patriarchal mindsets. Gang rape and merciless killing of a minor by RPF personnel in Kanpur Police station, Uttar Pradesh is a glaring example in which the complainant prayed for intervention of the Commission. As per the complaint, it was a well thought out plan as the father of the minor girl was jailed on frivolous charges and the mother had left the child in the home so as to visit her husband in the jail. The commission took cognizance of the matter[128] and issued directions to the Railway Board, Govt. of India and in pursuant of the directions of the Commission it was reported that a Crime case u/s 147/148/376/302 IPC had been registered against RPF constables Vinay Kumar singh and six others and during investigation, on the basis of evidence, RPF constable Vinay kumar singh was arrested and sent to jail. On completion of investigation charge sheet against three accused persons was filed in the court and they were placed under suspension. On examining all the facts of the case, the Commission observed that it prima facie showed that RPF constable/constables has/have committed rape of an 11 year old female children and later murdered her which was a clear violation of human rights and next of kin of the deceased child was entitled for monitory relief and accordingly the Commission recommended payment of Rs. 3,00,000/- to the next of kin of the deceased child by the Railway Board, Govt. of India.

In the Annual Report for the year 1999-2000, the Commission dealt in detail on the topic of 'Discrimination Based on Gender' and 'Discrimination Based on Caste'. While dealing with the former, it made important recommendations to overcome the issue of gender discrimination. In particular, it reiterated for the gender sensitisation of health workers, and a specifically targeted health care campaign to combat discrimination against girls and women. It further recommended the training of other key players in the governance of the country, such as, members of the judiciary, administration and police personnel to sensitive gender-related issues and the requirements of the

Constitution, and the laws and treaty commitments of the country. It strongly recommended that early action be taken at the political level for better representation for women in the State Legislatures and in the Parliament. It also reinforced that the National Reproductive and Child Health Programme be strengthened and that concerted efforts be made to bring down the rate of maternal mortality.

4. Focal Point on Human Rights of Women including Trafficking

Thereafter, in follow-up of a recommendation made by the Asia Pacific Forum of National Human Rights Institutions in a meeting held in Manila in September 1999, the United Nations High Commissioner for Human Rights requested each National Institution to nominate an appropriate individual to serve as a Focal Point on Human Rights of Women including Trafficking. Accordingly, the Commission, in 2001, designated one of its Members to serve as a Focal Point on Human Rights of Women including Trafficking. To make the people aware about the problem of trafficking, the Focal Point brought out an Information Kit on Trafficking in Women and Children. Subsequently, in order to create an authentic database to deal with the problem in all its dimensions, it undertook an Action Research on Trafficking in Women and Children in India along with the UNIFEM and the Institute of Social Sciences, a research organisation based at New Delhi. The main objective of the Action Research was to find out the trends and dimensions of trafficking, role of different law enforcement agencies in preventing and combating trafficking, process of rescue/recovery, rehabilitation and reintegration and role of other national institutions and the civil society in preventing and combating trafficking. The study also looked into the relationship between missing persons vs. trafficking, migration and trafficking, tourism and trafficking and culturally sanctioned practices and trafficking. The report of the Action Research was released to the general public on 24th of August 2004. The report has made some useful suggestions and recommendations to prevent and end trafficking. Based on these recommendations a Plan of Action to Prevent and End 'Tafficking in Women and children in India has been evolved by the Commission and disseminated to all concerned across the country. The Commission, ever since the Action Research was undertaken, has been continuously sensitising the judicial officers, police officers, administrative officers, functionaries of Homes, NGO representatives and the civil society at large. A network of Nodal Officers, two in each State - one from the Police Department and the other from the Social Welfare Department, has also been created to effectively deal with the problem of trafficking. Since trafficking is linked with sex tourism, the Commission in collaboration with the UNIFEM and a Mumbai based NGO organised a one-day sensitisation programme on Prevention of Sex Tourism and Trafficking in Mumbai in the year 2003. The primary objective of the programme was to sensitise senior representatives of the hotel and tourism industry on various issues relating to sex tourism and trafficking. In the year 2004, the Commission in collaboration with PRAYAS - a field action project of Tata Institute of Social Sciences, Mumbai organised a two-day National Workshop to Review the Implementation of Laws and Policies Related to Trafficking: Towards an Effective Rescue and Post-Rescue Strategies. The Commission held preliminary discussions with National Human Rights Commission of Nepal to combat cross-border trafficking. Steps were also taken with the help of an NGO based in Gorakhpur to prevent crossborder trafficking of women and children along the Indo-Nepal border.

Inspite of that, trafficking of women and girls still continues, both for sexual exploitations as well as for illegal labor, inspite of the Government initiatives like Ujjawala scheme. Sometimes the victims are poverty stricken and forced into the prostitution by their own parents. In one of such case the NHRC took suo motu cognizance of a news report about young girls being sold and forced into flesh trade by their own parents.[129] In the report submitted to the Commission by the director General of police, Hyderabad it was revealed that three criminal cases were registered in connection with the incident and 16 accused were arrested and 11 girls of which 5 were minor, were rescued. Since the problem of prostitution has its moorings in poverty in present case, the Commission made efforts to address the problem and the assistance of NGOs and other departments was taken in mitigating the menace and the minor girls were sent to the rehabilitation centers. The commission further called upon the Superintendent of Police, Kakinada to submit up-to-date report about action taken for rehabilitation of the victims.

5. Sexual Harassment

Sexual harassment of women at the work place and in trains is another area that has engrossed the attention of the Commission ever since the Focal Point on Human Rights of Women was constituted in 2001. Sexual harassment is an insidious form of violence against women's rights that not only harms a woman physically but also finishes her soul. While dealing with complaints of sexual harassment, the Commission observed that the guidelines issued by the Supreme Court in its landmark judgement in the case of **Vishaka v. State of Rajasthan** [1997 (6), SCC 241] were not being implemented adequately in institutions, whether falling under the public sector or the private sector. It also observed that many institutions had not yet set up the complaints mechanism, required under the judgement, to deal with complaints of sexual harassment at the work place. In order to consider and clarify these issues, the Commission convened several meetings with various Departments of the Government of India like the Department of Personnel and Training (DoPT), educational departments/institutions, such as the Department of Secondary and Higher Education, Department of Elementary Education and Literacy of the Ministry of Human Resource Development, University Grants Commission, Central Board of Secondary Education, Directorate of Education of the NCT of Delhi, besides meetings with the legal fraternity. It is with the intervention of the Commission that the role of the Complaints Committee prescribed in Vishaka Guidelines has been redefined. Complaints Committees are now deemed to be an inquiry authority for the purposes of the Central Civil Services (Conduct) Rules, 1964 and the report of the Complaints Committee shall be deemed to be an inquiry report under those Rules. The Commission has also been continuously monitoring the implementation of the Vishaka Guidelines in all States and Union Territories. Except for the State of Manipur, all the States have amended the Conduct Rules for their employees. Likewise, except for Sikkim, all the States and Union Territories have also constituted Complaints Committees to deal with complaints of sexual harassment against women. The Commission in 2005, also organised a workshop in New Delhi to sensitise the members of the Complaints Committees that have been constituted in the government departments to enable them to deal with the issue effectively. With regard to preventing and combating sexual harassment of female passengers in trains, it is working in close collaboration with the Ministry of Railways and a Delhi based non-governmental organisation. Through our collective efforts, FIR forms are now available in Hindi, English, Tamil,-Telugu, Marathi, Kannada and Malayalam languages with the mobile and stationary staff of railways. To enhance gendersensitivity among the railway officers and staff, a new capsule course of five-days duration has been evolved and training based on this new module has been imparted to different personnel of railways.

6. Rehabilitation of Destitute/Marginalised Women

The Commission has also been focussing on the plight of a large number of destitute/ marginalised women, especially widows languishing in peripheries of various temples in Vrindavan. In December 2000, two Members of the Commission visited Vrindavan and made an on the spot assessment of their situation which was found to be horrendous. The Commission then took up the issue with the Union Government (Ministry of Women and Child Development) and the State

Government of Uttar Pradesh. It has held several meetings with their representatives so that the basic necessities could be provided to these women for their sustenance in a dignified manner. In July 2003, a delegation led by the Focal Point of the Commission visited Vrindavan to review the situation. Though there was marked improvement in their situation, their overall situation was far from satisfactory. After this, a team led by the Joint Secretary of the Ministry of Women and Child Development visited Vrindavan in 2004 to see the overall progress made with regard to the sustenance of these women. Some of the notable achievements worth reporting are that a shelter home at Chaitanya Vihar Phase II for providing accommodation to about 500 destitute women is on the verge of completion. It is learnt that another NGO will also construct a shelter home in Vrindavan with assistance under the SWADHAR Scheme of Government of India. Regular medical camps are being held in Vrindavan to look after the medical needs of these women. Pension, though meagre, is being provided to most of these women. Ration cards have been provided to most of these women. LPG connections have also been provided for group cooking.

7. Population Policy and Women's Rights

In the light of the National Population Policy 2000 (NPP) and population policies framed by State Governments, the Commission decided to initiate a dialogue on them from the perspective of both development and human rights. Thus, in 2003, in collaboration with the Department of Family Welfare, Ministry of Health and Family Welfare and the United Nations Population Fund, organised a two-day Colloquium on Population Policy - Development and Human Rights. The participants to this Colloquium were administrators, policy-makers from State and Central Governments, human rights experts and representatives of non-governmental organisations working in the field. The Colloquium concluded by expressing concern that the population policies framed and rigorously implemented by some of the State Governments reflected a coercive approach through use of incentives and disincentives, which was inconsistent with the spirit of the NPP. Such an approach violated the rights of a large section of the population, especially the marginalised and the vulnerable, including women. The Colloquium therefore recommended that the State Governments/Union Territories exclude these discriminatory and coercive measures from population policies. To delve into the matter further, it has recently constituted a Working Group to examine the issue of incentives and disincentives in the Population Policies of the State Governments vis-a-vis the NPP.

8. Domestic Violence

Domestic violence is another issue which violates the dignity of women. To assess the ground realities, two research projects were undertaken by the Commission in this area. One of them pertained to Studying Complaints made by Women at Police Stations at Bangalore and the other was on Domestic Violence Against Women in India: Nature, Causes and Response of Criminal Justice System. The former was carried out along with an NGO and the latter with the National Police Academy at Hyderabad. Both these studies have confirmed that domestic violence perpetrated on women is a harshreality and the police did not pay much attention towards this problem. The Commission also examined the provisions of the Protection from Domestic Violence Bill 2002 along with the report containing the recommendations of the Standing Committee and forwarded its detailed suggestions to the Ministry of Women and Child Development. The Commission was indeed satisfied when it saw its suggestions were incorporated in the Protection of Women from Domestic Violence Act, 2005.

9. Other Issues and NHRC's Initiatives

Not only the sexual exploitation and trafficking of women but the overall liberty of women also appears to be at stake. In Hyderabad, three HIV positive siblings were refused admission by schools since the management of the schools were against accepting HIV positive children. These schools disregarded the order of the Andhra Pradesh government, that educational institutions should not discriminate against anyone and must admit HIV positive children. The youngest of the three siblings has already succumbed to HIV and the surviving two siblings are presently being tutored by an NGO. A case with respect to the right to education of these children is pending in the Andhra Pradesh High Court.[130] Unfortunately, our health system has failed to deal with communicable diseases and their effects on women in a gender sensitive way, which results in many women being denied treatment and becoming increasingly vulnerable to ill health. The structural inequalities must be addressed to curb the growth of emerging and re-emerging diseases. Interventions in communicable diseases must be planned with cognisance of the way in which gender influences the degree to which men and women, as individuals and as population groups, have access to and control of the resources needed to protect their own families and that of community members.[131] In another case of this line relating to arrest of an innocent woman by the police in place of an accused woman whose name was similar the NHRC took cognizance.[132] The commission directed the Secretary, Home, Chandigarh Administration to initiate Departmental Inquiry against the guilty police personnel. The commission recommended for their termination of service after adverse remarks received in the Departmental Inquiry against them.

Thus, a number of other programmes and issues relating to women were pursued intermittently by the Commission viz. the increase in the maintenance allowance for divorced women as provided for in section 125 Cr.P.C; the protection of the anonymity of victims of rape; the nomenclature to be used in official documents for addressing the wives of persons who have died; and the establishment of a Cell within the Commission to examine complaints received from women.

CHAPTER -V
RIGHTS OF CHILDERN

The 'rights of children', is another area that has drawn the attention of the Commission ever since it was constituted in October 1993. The Commission observed that despite there being major provisions in the Constitution of India for survival, development and protection of children as well as plethora of laws to safeguard their interests, the fact that the Government of India had ratified the United Nations Convention on the Rights of the Child (CRC), children all over the country, especially those belonging to weaker sections of the society, were found to be vulnerable and their dignity and human rights were often trampled. The initial few months of the Commission were thus spent on making an overall assessment about the range of issues concerning the rights of the child. Once this was accomplished, the Commission over the years focused its attention on child labour, child marriage, child trafficking and prostitution, child sexual violence, female foeticide and infanticide, child rape, HIV/AIDS afflicted children and juvenile justice.

1. Child Labour

The Commission, first and foremost, concentrated on issues of child labour, especially those employed in hazardous industries. In order to provide suitable remedies to the problem of child labour, it made a special effort to study the plight of these children employed in the glass work and carpet making industries of Uttar Pradesh, the beedi, match-sticks and fireworks industries in Tamil Nadu and the slate-pencil making industry in Madhya Pradesh. NHRC studied the glasswork industry in the district of Ferozabad, Uttar Pradesh, where some 50,000 children were reported to be working. The rehabilitation of these children was evolved as an integrated programme, involving the coordinated efforts of a number of- Central Ministries and the Government of Uttar Pradesh, and non-governmental organisations. The programme was based on three interrelated concepts: income-support for the families from where children went to work in the glass work industry; schooling for the children, creation of new facilities for children weaned away from employment; and rigorous implementation of the Child Labour (Prohibition and Regulation) Act 1986. On the issue of child labour, the Commission has consistently laid emphasis on the provision of free and compulsory education for children upto the age of 14 years, and the allocation of an appropriate level of resources to achieve this objective. The Right to Education, if fulfilled, would in itself be a strong weapon in the battle to end child labour.

The issue was of such critical significance to the Commission that the then Chairperson of the Commission addressed a letter on 11 January 1996 to the Presidents of all the major political parties in India. In it, he observed that despite the promise of Article 45 of the Constitution, 45 years after that noble document came into effect, one incontrovertible fact faces the nation: the number of those who are illiterate in the country exceeds the entire population of India at the time of independence. This grim reality enfeebles the country in every way, whether civil and political, or economic, social and cultural. It affects the dignity and self-esteem of countless Indians and exposes them to constant violations of their human rights. In its most aggravated form, this finds painful expression in tens of millions of our youth working as child labour, or even as bonded labour, in hazardous or utterly demeaning circumstances. The Chairperson thus urged that definite steps be taken to give comprehensive legislative backing to the Directive Principle contained in Article 45 of the Constitution. In response Department of Education deliberated on this matter and instead of all- India legislation on free and compulsory education, it chose to adopt a different strategy to achieve the goal of the "universalization of elementary education". It is due to Commission's continued efforts that education has today become a Fundamental:Right for the children between the age group of 6 and 14 years through 86th Amendment of the Constitution.

To end the scourge of child labour from the country, the Commission's efforts have also been directed towards generating greater awareness and sensitivity in the District Administration and Labour Departments of concerned States. Based on the feedback of the Special Rapporteur entrusted with the task of monitoring the issue of child labour, the Commission has from time to time issued specific directions to the State Government in respect of the detection and withdrawal of children employed in hazardous occupation/processes, the admission of such children into the formal and non-formal system of schooling, particularly the schools established under the National Child Labour Project, the economic rehabilitation of the affected families, and the prosecution of offending employers. It also undertook a study on the 'Impact Community Response and Acceptance of Non-formal Education under the National Child Labour Project' in the carpet weaving districts and glass bangles region of Ferozabad in Uttar Pradesh.

2. Children as Domestic Help

In 1996-97, the Commission received disturbing reports of the employment of children below the age of 14 years as domestic servants in the homes of government officials. Unacceptable as the practice is in any circumstance, the Commission felt that the employment of such children as domestic help in the homes of government officials was particularly reprehensible. Following a meeting in January 1996, the Commission decided to recommend that an appropriate rule be included in the conduct rules of government servants, both Central and States, which while prohibiting such employment would also make it a misconduct inviting a major penalty. The Commission accordingly requested the Minister of State in the Ministry of Personnel, Public Grievances and Pensions to take appropriate steps to introduce the rule in to the Government Service (Conduct) Rules 1964, and proposed the precise wording required for this purpose. This view of the Commission effected necessary amendments to Conduct Rules of the Central and State Government servants. By virtue of these amendments, employment of children below 14 years by the government servants as domestic help now attracts disciplinary action.

3. Child Marriage

The widespread persistence of child marriage in certain parts of the country coaxed the Commission to examine this problem in its enormity. On examination of the problem, the Commission realised that the Child Marriage Restraint Act, 1929 (CMRA) should be recast so as to provide for higher penalty for the violations of the provisions mass-scale awareness programmes/campaigns, in association with the Integrated Child Development Services, local self-governments/Panchayats and Legal Service Authorities to educate and sensitise people about the demerits of child marriages.

4. Child Trafficking and Prostitution

Alerted by press reports to the alarming increase in child trafficking and prostitution in Tamil Nadu and Goa in the year 1995-96, the Commission issued notice to the two State Governments as well as to the Department of Women and Child Development, Government of India, calling for reports on the situation. Simultaneously, it also decided to have this issue considered on a regular basis by a Core Group, consisting of representatives from the National Commission for Women, the Department of Women and Child Development, UNICEF and selected NGOs. The Core Group reviewed the existing laws and ways of improving their enforcement; it discussed the efforts made and difficulties faced in rehabilitating children weaned away from prostitution; it pressed for greater efforts at the level of SAARC, to strengthen laws and to devise cooperative measures to deal with trans-border movements; and encouraged organisation of workshops and hearings by individual members of the Core Group.

Given the global ramifications of this problem, the Commission also represented at the First World Congress Against Commercial Sexual Exploitation of Children that was held in Stockholm from 26-31 August 1996. Later in the year 2002, the Commission embarked on an Action Research on Trafficking in Women and Children in India in order to know the magnitude, trends and dimensions of the problem of trafficking. The report of the Action Research has brought forth startling facts, such as children are trafficked not only for commercial sexual exploitation but also for various other purposes. Further, the Commission and the Ministry of Women and Child Development, Government of India in partnership with UNICEF have prepared a Manual for the Judicial Workers on Combating Trafficking of Women and Children for Commercial Sexual Exploitation. The purpose of the manual is to sensitise the judicial officers to however of the view that in order to further bring about awareness among the people at large, the electronic media too would have to be involved and mobilised. As a result, the NHRC, in partnership with Prasar Bharati and UNICEF held four workshops for radio and television producers. The participants for these workshops were drawn from 20 States. It was during the course of these workshops that an idea of bringing out a guidebook for the media to address the issue of sexual violence against children emerged. Based on the deliberations of these workshops, the Commission and the Prasar Bharati, with support from UNICEF, jointly prepared A Guidebook for the Media on Sexual Violence Against Children. The main objective of the guidebook is to encourage media professionals to address the issue of sexual violence against children in a consistent, sensitive and effective manner, consonant with the rights and best interest of children. The Commission currently is also in the process of preparing guidelines for speedy disposal of child rape cases. Both the actual situation of the trafficked victims and to provide them with a perspective so that they could proactively safeguard the rights of victimised women and children, through a sensitive interpretation of the law.

5. Sexual Violence Against Children

Sexual violence against children is another sensitive issue in which the Commission took concrete measures. Pained with the plight of child victims, visa-vis the manner in which the issue was being reported by the media, the Commission decided to intervene in the matter in the year 1998, when a two-month campaign was launched in New Delhi in collaboration with the Department of Women and Child Development, UNICEF and non-governmental organisations. A mid-term appraisal of the campaign revealed that irrespective of the medium, message or location, the campaign effectively raised awareness about sexual violence against children. The respondents were of this Act and also to make the offence cognizable and non-bailable. In December 1999, it also considered the question of whether it would be preferable to provide for compulsory registration of marriages in the Hindu Marriage Act, 1955 through appropriate amendments, instead of making such a provision in the CMRA. This was also discussed with the Secretary, Legislative Department in September 2000 wherein it was suggested by him to gather information as to how many States had made rules under section 8 of the Hindu Marriage Act. The Chief Secretaries of all the States were accordingly requested to send the requisite information; However, after considering the entire issue, the Commission decided to review the CMRA. It thus reviewed the CMRA and recommended to the Government of India a number of amendments to it. In pursuance of these recommendations, the Government of India introduced "The Prevention of Child Marriage Bill" in the Rajya Sabha on 20th of December 2004, incorporating all the recommendations of the Commission. The Bill was under the examination of the Department Related Parliamentary Standing Committee on Personnel, Public Grievances, Law and Justice. The proposed Bill on becoming an Act would go a long way in curbing the child marriage in the country. Pending the passage of the Bill into an Act, the Commission has written to concerned Ministries/Departments in the Central Government and the State Governments/Union Territories to organise

6. Female Foeticide and Infanticide

Faced with the widely prevalent misuse of sex determination tests to commit female foeticide, the Commission approached the Medical Council of India during the year 1995-96, to take a position on the ethical aspects of such tests. After reviewing the matter, the Council decided to suggest suitable amendments to the regulations governing the code of medical ethics, in order to enable undertaking of disciplinary proceedings against errant doctors. Thereafter, the issue of 'discrimination' as a cause of human rights violations was examined in great detail in the Commission's Annual Report for 1999-2000, especially in relation to gender and caste-based discrimination. In the light of recommendations made by the CRC Committee in its concluding observations with regard to the report on children submitted by the Government of India, the Commission reiterated that there was an urgent need to ensure that free and compulsory education was provided as a fundamental right to all children until they completed that age of 14 years. It also emphasised the need for undertaking a vigorous and comprehensive national campaign against female foeticide and infanticide.

During the course of regional and national consultations on Public Health and Human Rights that were held during 2002-03, the Commission again took up the issue of combating female foeticide and infanticide. The issue featured again when the Commission organised a Colloquium on Population Policy - Development and Human Rights in January 2003. To counter this problem, the Commission has maintained that vigorous and comprehensive measures be taken by all States and Union Territories to put an end to the gruesome problem of female foeticide and infanticide.

7. Right to Health of Children

The violation of the rights of children has also been considered from the angle of health. In 2000 and 2001, the Commission organised a workshop on Human Rights and HIV/ AIDS that was followed by a consultation on Public Health and Human Rights. these had direct relevance to the rights of children. Later, in the year 2004, the Chairperson of the Commission addressed letters to the Union Ministers for Human Resource Development, Health and Chief Ministers of All States/Union Territories urging them to take steps to prevent discrimination of children affected by HIV/AIDS with regard to access to education and health care. In particular, the Commission asked them to enact and enforce a legislation to prevent children living with HIV/AIDS from being discriminated against, including being barred from school.

8. Juvenile Justice

Deeply concerned with the plight of juveniles in the country, the Commission in 1996 wrote letters to Chief Secretaries/Administrators of all States/Union Territories on the reporting of deaths/rapes in Juvenile/Children's Homes within 24 hours. Since some of the Homes were not found to be functioning properly, the Commission once again directed to the Chief Secretaries/Administrators of all States/Union Territories to ensure prompt communication of incidents of custodial deaths/rapes in Juvenile/ Children's Homes. Later, when the Juvenile Justice Act, 1986 was repealed by the Juvenile Justice (Care and Protection of Children) Act, 2000, the Commission was deeply concerned over the poor implementation of this Act. As such, it devised a format seeking information regarding implementation of the various provisions of the 2000 Act. It has also entrusted a research study on the subject to a non-governmental organisation. The study on completion will suggest measures for better implementation of the Act.

9. Optional Protocols to the Convention on the Rights of the Child

The Commission has vigorously pursued with the Government of India to ratify the two Optional Protocols to the CRC, viz. the Optional Protocol to the Convention on the Rights of the Child on the Involvement of Children in Armed Conflict and the Optional Protocol to the Convention on the Rights of the Child on the Sale of Children, Child Prostitution and Child Pornography. Accordingly, the Government of India ratified the latter Protocol on 16th of August 2005 and the former Optional Protocol on 30th of November 2005.

CHAPTER -VI
RIGHTS OF THE DALITS

The Commission has been actively engaged since its inception in the protection and promotion of the human rights of Dalits. The Commission has viewed its role as that of an "Equalizer" adding its weight on behalf of the vulnerable, so that the scales of justice and equity may be more evenly balanced for them, and to ensure that those who violate the rights of the vulnerable are brought to justice, as the Constitution of the country, its laws and treaty obligations all require.

1. Redressal of Complaints

The Commission besides on complaints has also acted as suo moto in number of cases to address the human rights violations of Dalits and to ensure that rights of the disadvantaged were protected and respected. The number of complaints of atrocities against SCs and STs, received and admitted by this Commission was 552 in 1997-98, 436 in 1998-99 and 736 in 1999-2000. In Year 2005 the Commission registered 1597 complaints and the Commission disposed off 1994 complaints, similarly upto 19 June 19, 2006 Commission registered 894 complaints NHRC. The Workshop noted that, despite the existence of the Protection of Civil Rights Act, 1976, the violation of human rights of dalits had increased. The implementation of the Act left much to be desired; investigations into atrocities against dalits were often "inadequate" or biased. The Workshop also noted that the conviction rate of perpetrators of atrocities against dalits was very low and that there was need to plug the loopholes that permitted this. Mention was, very often, made to the frequency of atrocities resulting from disputes over land, and the need to implement land reforms diligently. Above all, the workshop called for greater sensitization of all the agencies of Government, the judiciary and law enforcement machinery in particular, to the special problems posed in protecting the rights of dalits. It was the first major dialogue that the Commission had initiated in respect of societal violations of human rights of an important and particularly vulnerable section of the population of this country.

2. Eradication of Manual Scavenging

One of the important issues taken up by the Commission since then has been the campaign to end manual scavenging. The Commission has pursued this issue with the State Governments and with the Centre seeking to bring this deeply demeaning practice to an early end. Intervention of the Commission with Central and State Governments Construction of Dry Latrines (Prohibition) Act, 1993 on 24th January 1997. The Planning Commission has also formulated a National Action Plan for total Eradication of Manual Scavenging by 2007.Thus, the Commission has been vigorously pursuing the need to end the degrading practice of manual scavenging in the country. The Commission has taken up this matter at the highest echelons of the Central and State Governments through a series of personal interventions by the Chairperson of the Commission. The Commission, on its part, too has urged all the State Governments and Union Territories to work with greater determination to implement the Act so as to ensure that the dehumanizing practice can be effectively stopped. The Commission held a number of meetings with the State Governments. The last such meeting was held on 25 February 2006 on Eradication of Manual Scavenging under the Chair of the Hon'ble Chairperson, NHRC with the representatives of Central and the State Governments and other stakeholders.

3. Rooting out Untouchability

In order to root out the untouchability the Commission recommended that the Government of India undertake comprehensive steps to root out 'Untouchability' and, for this purpose, implement the provisions of the Protection of Civil Rights Act, 1976 and the Prevention of Atrocities against SCs and STs Act, 1989 more vigorously than hitherto. The Commission sought to bring to an end two pernicious and demeaning practices which affected members of the Scheduled Castes and Scheduled Tribes in large measure: manual scavenging and bonded labour. The former issue was first taken up by the Commission in 1996-97. In recent years, it has been the matter of successive communications at the highest level from Chairpersons of the Commission to the Prime Minister of India and the Chief Ministers of States. The Commission is of the firm view that there is a need to combat age-old biases and entrenched attitudes through education and through public information campaigns. NHRC in collaboration with Kamataka Women's Information and Resource Centre, KWIRC, Bangalore is working on Project for developing resource materials for Human Rights Education in Indian Universities, which also includes dossier on Dalit rights - migration in search of labour and other experiences of Dalits. The Commission has also been taking up research studies on issues concerning dalits in this direction. The Commission also granted financial assistance to Maharishi Dayanand University, Rohtak, Haryana to carry out a pilot study on the socio economic, political and cultural status of dalit women in Haryana.

The Crime Against Scheduled Castes has also been a historical fact and continues to be an unfortunate feature of contemporary India. In other words, the violation of the customary rules and practices invite violent crime against the dalits by other castes. This feature of strong exclusion for the enforcement of caste system plays an important role in continuity of the system despite the changes in the legal framework in contemporary India. The Country has made measurable progress in terms of the protections afforded to Dalits since independence; however, Dalits still suffer discrimination and mistreatment, which is inexcusable under both domestic laws and Country's obligations under international law. The crimes committed against the Scheduled Castes remain a cause of great concern to the Commission. The Commission has been actively engaged since its inception in the protection and promotion of the human rights of Dalits. The Commission has viewed its role as that of an "Equalizer" adding its weight on behalf of the vulnerable, so that the scales of justice and equity may be more evenly balanced for them, and to ensure that those who violate the rights of the vulnerable are brought to justice, as the Constitution of the country, its laws and treaty obligations all require." In order to root out untouchability the Commission recommended that the Government of India to undertake comprehensive steps to root out 'Untouchability' and requires implementation of the Protection of Civil Rights Act, 1976 and the Prevention of Atrocities Against SCs and STs Act, 1989 more vigorously. The Commission was convinced that, the Constitution has shown the way, Legislative and affirmative action programmes are firmly in place, but unquestionably need to be far better implemented.

Besides the Constitutional guarantees against caste based discrimination and Legislative and affirmative action programmes firmly in place, violence against Dalits is still persisting in various parts of the country. The districts identified above need more vigilance and monitoring from the concerned authorities to curb violence against Dalits. There is also strong need to aware and sensitize people to give up social and other disabilities against SCs. In areas where cases are large the appointment of exclusive special courts and appointment of competent and committed special public prosecutors will be helpful in bringing to justice those who are responsible for various criminal activities against dalits.

4. Training Programmes with NGOs

The Commission has also conducted many training programmes related with Dalit Rights with different NGOs from time to time. For example, Programme to sensitize the police personnel on issues of atrocities against Dalits in partnership with Indian Social Institute, Delhi; Role of Criminal Justice System in the Protection of Dalit

Rights, organised by Tata Institute of Social Sciences (TISS); 'Police Civil Society Interface for Promotion of Human Rights', Mumbai; TOT for NGOs to spread for legal literacy among women, poor and disadvantages/ target groups, Organised by Institute, Multiple Action Research Group (MARG), at Jhabua M.P.; Training Programme on Human Rights and Weaker Sections at Bhopal M.P.[133]

CHAPTER -VII
RIGHTS OF THE UNDERPREVILEGED SECTIONS

- **RIGHTS OF THE TRIBALSAND NHRC**

Since its inception, the Commission has been particularly engaged, suo motu or on the basis of complaints, with instances of various atrocities meted out against the vulnerable sections belonging to the Scheduled Castes and Scheduled Tribes. In this endeavour, the Chairpersons of the National Commission assisted the Commission for Minorities, the National Commission for Scheduled Castes & Scheduled Tribes and the National Commission for Women. The Commission also undertook the responsibility of promoting research in the field of human rights, with rights of the tribal women as one of its major prerogative. In the year 1995 - 96, the Commission received two major complaints with regard to children belonging to tribal communities - one was the torture and sexual assault of a minor tribal girl from Bihar in Maharashtra and the other one related to some tribal youths being stripped and forced to spend two nights in the police lock-up in Kerela. In the former case, the "Commission provided some interim financial assistance to the minor adivasi girl through an NGO in Ranchi. In the latter case, the state government of Kerela, keeping in line with the recommendations of the Commission, sanctioned necessary compensation to each of the victims.

In the year 1996 - 97, the Commission investigated the circumstances that compelled the tribals to leave their place of inhabitation from the site of Bargi Dam on the river Narmada. In August 1996, the Commission received a complaint from the National Alliance of People's Movements, requesting the intervention of the Commission in a "matter relating to the human rights violation of the Bargi Dam outsees of Madhya Pradesh." It was contended in the complaint that the lives and livelihood of several thousand families, many of whom were tribals, were in "immediate and grave danger" as a result of an official decision to raise the water level in the dam from 418 metres to 422.76 metres. At the policy level, the Commission recommended that the Central and State Governments re-examine and appropriately amend their laws, regulations and practices in order to ensure that, when it comes to acquisition of land for purposes related to national economic development, the provisions of the Constitution, as. expounded by the Supreme Court and as contained in international instruments to which India is a party, notably ILO Convention 107, are fully respected. The Commission considered it to be essential if the 'national' Interest was to be reconciled with true respect for the rights of the weakest sections of the society.

The Commission, in the year 1997-98, mentioned it clearly that where the petitioners belong to the vulnerable sections of the society, scheduled castes and scheduled tribes being one of them, those complaints should be treated on an urgent basis. It is worth mentioning that the communities designated as Denotified Tribes (DNT) and Nomadic Tribes (NT) of India were identified as 'Criminal Tribes' (which included both castes as well as tribes) in pre-independence India. Though the Criminal Tnbes Act, 1871 was annulled soon after independence the police, as well as members of the public, frequently and most regrettably continue to treat persons belonging to these communities as 'born criminals' and 'habitual criminals'. They therefore remain themost disadvantaged and discriminated ones in the country. The eminent activist and author, Smt. Mahasvetadevi, President, Denotified and Nomadic Tribals Rights Action Group, sent a petition to the Commission on the plight of the Denotified and Nomadic Tribal Communities of India referring to their ill treatment by the administration, and by the police in particular. Following the petition received from the Denotified and Nomadic tribal Rights Action Group which highlighted many instances of moblynching, arson and police brutality against members of the Denotified Tribes, the National Human Rights Commission constituted an advisory group on denotified and nomadic tribes in May 1998, to deal with these issues. In the same year under review, the commission received a complaint alleging about the harassment and torture of van gujjars by forest officials in Uttar Pradesh. The Commission intervened into this matter and accordingly made certain recommendations to protect the interests of the gujjars. On 15th February 2000, the Commission held a high level meeting to discuss the specific problems of denotified tribes and nomadic tribes. It was decided that there is a need to have a proper enumeration of denotified tribes and nomadic tribes throughout the country including even those who have merged into SC/ST/OBC categories. Their mere merging into these categories should not be an obstacle in their access to education, employment and other infra-structural facilities to them. The role of entire state machinery, especially the police officers were also taken into consideration. The commission recommends that the police officers needs to be sensitised about the problems of these tribes. In this direction the commission also took up the measure of providing appropriate training programme in the National Police Academy. An effort to survey the socio-economic conditions of the tribes was also suggested in order to be able to locate their specific problems.

Further, A complaint from Swami Agnivesh, who stated that tribals residing in the districts of Chitrakoot, Allahabad, Mirzapur and adjoining areas had not been given the status of scheduled tribes by the State Government and that this had deprived them of benefits to which they should have been entitled. The tribals had been living in poor economic conditions, held in bondage and forced to work in slave-like conditions, wages being paid to them being far below the minimum fixed by the Government. On considering the complaint the Commission was of the view that there was need for a radical change in the way in which the State Government dealt with the problems facing the tribals. There was need to recognize their special relationship with the forests and to fulfil the mandatory role of the State to enhance their well-being rather than to drive them out of the forest. The Commission also took the view that the existing system of auction of mining rights was totally unjust and led to the exploitation of the tribals.In the year 2000-01, the Commission had urged greater sensitivity at the highest political and administrative level to the problems of the tribes. The central government conveyed all the recommendations of the Commission to the concerned state government. In addition to this, the denotified tribes and nomadic tribes included in the list of SC were concerned; the government had already enacted a special Act, namely, the Scheduled Castes and Scheduled Tribes (Prevention of Atrocities) Act, 1989 to protect them against atrocities.

The Commission also took suo motu cognisance of a news item published in the Hindu of 22 January 2000, which highlighted the suffering of women of the Lambada Tribe of Telangana Region in Andhra Pradesh. It was reported that, in a number of instances, they were being compelled by their circumstances either to sell or to kill their infant girls soon after birth. A detailed report, obtained by the Commission from Andhra Pradesh Government confirmed that there were numerous cases where the girl child was being given away, either for adoption, or sold. In many cases, neither the names nor the addresses of the persons supposedly adopting the children were known. The Commission took a serious view of this matter and observed that the Supreme Court of India had laid down clear guidelines in respect of the adoption of Indian children by foreign nationals. Unfortunately, in most of such cases, poverty and illiteracy were the main causes for the giving-up of the child. The Commission considered the issue in a meeting on

26 April 2001 and further directions were given to the State Government. The State Government subsequently sent a detailed report indicating how it would deal with the problem. In the light of that report, the Commission closed the proceedings before it. However, at the request of Smt. Shanti Reddy, a Member of the National Commission for Women, a high-level meeting was convened by the Commission where the Joint Secretary, Ministry of Social Justice and Empowerment and Director, Central Adoption Resource Agency (CARA) were present. The officials present agreed to review cases where foreign parents were not found suitable in adopting such babies.

- **RIGHTS OF THE DISABLED AND NHRC**

Equality, dignity, liberty are the founding principles on which International Human Rights law is premised. These values have sufficiently influenced the fundamental law of democratic polity and are reflected in constitutions of most democratic states including India. Under Right to Equality, the Constitution of India guarantees to all citizens equality before law and equal protection of law on grounds of religion, race, sex, caste, place of birth or any of them. The format recognition of discrimination on grounds of disability is a recent phenomena and laws enacted even 20 years ago generally did not include disability in the list of prohibited discrimination. The preamble of Persons with Disabilities (Equal opportunities, protection of rights and full participation Act, 1995 clearly delineates its objectives of promoting and ensuring equality and full'participation of persons with disabilities The act aims to protect and promote economic and social rights of people with disabilities. According to the Census of-India 2001, the total number of disabled in India constitutes more than 2 percent of the total population. Persons with disabilities (PWDs) are those who suffer from physical, mental or psychological impairment of varying degrees, either temporarily or permanently. This includes persons with blindness, hearing impairment, locomotor disability, cerebral palsy and multiple disabilities. Their lives are often handicapped due to various social, cultural, economic, infra structural and above all, attitudinal barriers which, acts as a stumbling block in their access to opportunities and their capacity to enjoy rights on an equal basis.

The National Human Rights Commission strongly holds the view that the rights of the people with disabilities needs to be protected, their dignity needs to be restored and their difference of ability needs to be recognized if the society is committed to give them an equal platform to contribute potentially to the life of the nation. In this endeavour, the Commission in the year 1993-94 had included in its agenda the issue of disability in terms of the atrocities committed against them. The first case that the Commission took cognizance of was the forced hystectomy without obtaining the consent of mentally challenged woman in Maharashtra. The Commission felt that the issue raised the question of the rights of persons suffering from mental disabilities and decided to obtain the views of the Medical Council of India. In the year 1994-95, the Commission expressed its concern for the prisoners with mental disabilities by making recommendations for the classification of the prisoners so that the mentally disabled are identified in this process and henceforth, special arrangements/ facilities are made available to them in the prisons. In addition to this, the Commission also recommended for the proper training and re-orientation of the prison staff in order to make them sensitive about the rights of the disabled. It also included visit to homes to check the living conditions of the prisoners. Being dissatisfied with the ineffective implementation of the Persons with Disability (Equal Opportunities, Protection of Rights and Full Participation) Act, 1995, the Commission sought information from the State governments regarding the measures that were implemented such as job reservation, reservation in admission to various educational institution, conveyance allowances, petrol subsidy, assistance for purchasing aids, loans for employment, special reservations in the allotment of government quarters for the benefit of the disabled persons. It also directed that the Chief Commissioner for persons with disabilities at the centra level and Commissioners for disabilities at the state level have to be in position, on a full time basis, to deal with the various issues related to the implementation of the Act in one of its measures to prevent death by starvation in Orissa, the Commission put forth its recommendation for providing disability pensions. The extent of social security net available to disabled persons was expanded on Commission's recommendations and the disbursement of disability pension under various schemes was streamlined. Amendment to the Persons with Disability (Equal Opportunities, Protection of Rights and Full Participation) Act, 1995.

Another task that the Commission took in the year 2000-01 with regard to the disabled is certain amendments regarding the Persons with Disability (Equal Opportunities, Protection of Rights and Full Participation) Act, 1995 for further strengthening of the Act and to pluck the loop holes inherent in it. In order to remove ambiguities in certain aspects of the Act and for its better implementation, the Commission has enlarged the definition of disability by including those persons who experience physical, intellectual or psychological impairment of varying degrees, either temporarily or permanently, and whose lives are handicapped by social, cultural, attitudinal and structural barriers, which hamper their freedom of participation, access to opportunities and enjoyment of rights on equal terms. The other suggestions covered inter-alia, the definition of a disability, the composition of Central and State Coordination Committees, reservation in jobs for persons with mental retardation, better access to facilities for persons with sensory disability and provisions relating to non-discrimination, care and protection.

The Commission has also successfully championed the need to enumerate the disabled in Census 2001. In order to give a focused attention to the rights of the disabled, a core group on disability was constituted by the Commission in August 2001, with Shri B.L. Sharma,

IAS (Retd) former Chief Commissioner of disabilities, as its chairperson. The core group was entrusted to consider the problems faced by the disabled from a human rights perspective and to evolve suitable ways and means of improving the conditions of the disabled. Working towards an effective implementation of the Persons with Disability (Equal Opportunities, Protection of Rights and Full Participation) Act, 1995, the Commission in the year 2002-03, made recommendations to both Union Ministers and Chief Ministers of all States and Union Territories to evolve a State Disability Policy and Plan of Action, in order to provide social security, employment opportunities, rehabilitation and barrier-free infrastructure to benefit the disabled. The Commission also adopted an in-house disability policy and an agenda for action. In this process, the disability perspective was incorporated in all aspects of the work undertaken by the Commission. For example, in all the training materials for public servants, an effort was being made to introduce an outline on the rights of persons with disabilities and the obligations of the various authorities of the State.

The Commission is also mandated under section 12 of the Protection of Human Rights Act to visit the Government run Mental Hospitals to "study the living conditions of the inmates and make recommendations thereon". Besides discharging this specific responsibility, the Commission has been, right from its inception, giving special attention to the human rights of the mental patients because of their vulnerability and need for special protection. The most notable intervention of the NHRC in mental health has been a project on 'Quality Assurance in Mental Health' launched in 1997. The project team headed by Dr. S.M. Channabasavanna, former Director NIMHANS worked under the overall guidance of Justice V.S. Malimath, Member NHRC. The ten member team comprised the Chairperson and 4 members from the Deptt. of Psychiatry and one member each from the Departments of Clinical Psychology, Nursing, Psychiatric Socio-work, Health Education and Neurological Rehabilitation. The main aim of the project was to analyse the conditions generally prevailing in Government run Mental Hospitals in various parts of the country with reference to infrastructure, patient care, admission, discharge and appeal procedure, rehabilitation facilities, client satisfaction and morale of the staff. The project team surveyed all the 37 Government run Mental Hospitals and actually visited 33 of them. It also considered comprehensive information collected from the Psychiatric Departments of some of the Medical Colleges. It organised Zonal meetings at Bangalore, Agra, Ahmedabad and Kolkata which were attended by NGOs, mental patients and their family members besides the mental health professionals. A series of workshops for selected staff from each hospital were also held to enhance the sensitivity of the key Administrators and impart special skill and orientation to the staff at the functional level. The project report submitted in June 1999 makes comprehensive recommendations in respect of each of the 37 Government run Mental Hospitals along with useful suggestions for action at the State level.

In addition to the above-mentioned steps taken by the Commission to ensure rights for the disabled persons, it has also through various conferences, publications, cases and research studies tried to spread awareness of the rights of the disabled.

- ### RIGHTS OF INTERNALLY DISPLACED PERSONS AND NHRC

The National Human Rights Commission has on number of occasions taken cognizance of the plight of internally displaced persons (IDPs) induced by the natural disasters, mega development projects and other reasons. These types of situations have increased its importance when there is already the lack of effective legal framework to deal with the problem of IDPs. Similarly, role of the NHRC becomes much wider when the state authorities show inadequate response in dispensation of relief and other humanitarian assistance to the IDPs. As such there is no legal definition for internally displaced persons as there is for refugees. According to 1951 Convention on Status of Refugees a "Refugee" is a person who, "owing to well founded fear of being persecuted for reasons of race, religion, nationality, membership of a particular social group or political opinion, is outside the country of his nationality and is unable, or owing to such fear, is unwilling to avail himself of the protection of that country; or who, not having a nationality and being outside the country of his former habitual residence as a result of such events, is unable or, owing to such fear, is unwilling to return to it". Unlike refugees, the IDPs do not have a special status in the international law with rights specific to their concern. Until early 1990s, no definition on "internally displaced persons" existed. A starting point in this direction was the working definition of that had been put forth in 1992 by the United Nations Secretary-General Boutros-Ghali, which defines internally displaced person as: "persons or groups who have been forced to flee their homes suddenly or unexpectedly in large numbers, as a result of armed conflict, internal strife, systematic violations of human rights or natural or man-made disaster, and who are within the territory of their own country".[134] The more recent definition, which is widely accepted, is coined by Mr. Francis Deng and other International Legal Experts is mentioned in the 1998 UN Guiding Principles on internal Displacements. The Guiding Principles define the internally displaced persons as "persons or group of persons who have been forced or obliged to flee or to leave their homes or places of habitual residence, in particular as a result of or in order to avoid the effects of armed conflict, situations of generalised violence, violation of human rights or natural or human made disasters, and who have not crossed an internationally recognised state border. The Asia Pacific Forum on Human Rights in its 10th Annual Meeting in Ulaanbaatar, Mongolia also recognized that there is need to protect and promote the rights of the IDPs in line with the UN Guiding Principles on IDPs. The guidelines developed by the Asia Pacific Forum on IDPs entitled "Guidelines on Internally Displaced Persons in the Context of the Natural Disasters: a Common Methodology for National Human Rights Institutions" in its preamble also mentions that "IDPs are distinguished from other persons by common types of vulnerability that displacement exposes them to as well as by their need for a durable solution to that displacement. Displacement frequently entails consequences such as increased vulnerability to physical violence, in particular sexual and gender-violence; psychological trauma; lack of basic necessities of life (e.g. food, water, shelter, clothing sanitation); disease and impoverishment; and other difficulties". It was 28th October 2005, that APF in Colombo adopted the guidelines on IDPs in the "Regional Workshop on National Human Rights Institutions and Internally Displaced Persons". The participants of the workshop recognise the three primary causes of internal displacement in the Asian region: conflict, natural disaster and development projects. The Participants also urge Governments to acknowledge the different types of displacement, whether by conflict, communal strife, natural disaster or development projects, and take steps to address the human rights dimension of the problem without discrimination of any kind, including on the basis of ethnic origin, caste, gender, religion, legal status, political or other persuasion or between those displaced by conflict and natural disaster. It is important to recognise such peoples as IDPs entitled to the rights contained in the UN Guiding Principles on Internal Displacement.

The NHRC is of the opinion that the resettlement and rehabilitation of persons displaced through the acquisition of land for various projects should form part of the provisions of the Land Acquisition Act, 1894 itself, or be the subject of appropriate separate legislation. The Commission was additionally of the view that the Government should, while adopting a comprehensive policy, provide for that policy to itself be incorporated into appropriate legislation within a specified time frame to make it justiciable. Lastly, it is worth to mention that UN Guiding Principles do no exclude those who are being displaced by development projects, as Principle 6(c) of these Principles prohibits arbitrary displacement in cases of large-scale developments. However, need is to make a comprehensive definition on IDPs, which will include all those who are being displaced by mega-development projects. Over the past five years, a number of governments and regional bodies have begun to adopt policies and laws on internal displacement and five other countries are in the process of doing so. It is expected that these policies and laws will enlighten further in drafting guidelines as per the National needs.

Hence, it can be seen that human rights, in any society, are intrinsic in human nature and they are completely essential for living as a human being. Human rights are the foundation of human life, self-respect and worth. Human rights can be elaborated as the condition by which man can archive self-freedom and can make the fullest development of him. Human Rights create specific conditions to help an individual to develop his persona. To live the life of dignity of the personality, to express his thoughts freely, to get the freedom to follow any religious dogmas, to make any business and for the financial and educational development as well as the political participation, human rights are more indispensable for human being. The NHRC of India has tried to be comprehensive in its functioning in this direction.

- **WAY FORWARD**

It can be seen from overall analysis that the role of NHRC of india is seen as complementary to that of the government, the judiciary and other institutions within the State involved in promoting and protecting human rights standards. The Rule of Law is indispensable for the exercise of the Government in a way that promotes and protects Human Rights. A number of Declarations, Covenants and Legislations have been imitated and entered into the National and International levels for the effective promotion and protection of Human Rights. Respect for the dignity of an individual and striving for peace and harmony in society has been an abiding factor in Indian culture. Thus, these rights must have a social respect and must be enforceable by the state government. However the violation of Human Rights has been increasing day by day. Hence Human Rights enforcement mechanism has been established to enforce Human Rights at the national and International levels. Today, there is a need of strong society based on the fundamental principles of acceptance of Human Rights both in theory as well as in practice. Therefore, this Book aims to look at the public legitimacy of the National Human Rights Institutions, rather than mere formal legitimacy contained in Law: Whether it is independent of Government, whether it has a mandate to tackle the sensitive human rights issues and whether its finding has any effect? While analyzing the role and functioning of the Commission, the focus has also been upon its political will: Whether it is prepared to tackle the difficult issues that would put it into conflict with the Government? Woulld it address the needs of the victims of human rights violations and the priorities of civil society institutions?

The Constitution creats Fundamental Rights for the people and also prescribes Directive Principles of State Policy together, designed to create equality and equal protection of laws for all. Fundamental Rights Part which is made justiciable, cast the responsibility of enforcing these freedoms on the judiciary. An overloaded judicial system, a legacy of the past, rose to the occasion and gave memorable judgments, upholding Constitutional values and protecting individuals against violations of their freedom by the State. But the new responsibility added a crushing case load on already overloaded Courts. Therefore, it is imperative to establish other concurrent systems for the protection of human rights.

At international level, the UN Commission on Human Rights framed the Universal Declaration of Human Rights (UDHR) and it was approved by the United Nations General Assembly in 1948. The UDHR desires member nations to promote a number of human, civil, economic and social rights. The international community has acknowledged the mounting importance of strengthening national human rights institutions. In this background, the ACHPR and the Paris Principles provided for the creation of 'National Human Rights Institutions' [NHRIs]; whose establishment will strengthen the existing mechanism of protecting human rights. The national character of such institutions enables them to de-mystify universal principles and translate them into practical measures at the level where it most matters. [135]

The analysis of the Paris Principles and the NHRI concept leads to three main conclusions. First, the Paris Principles –originally dubbed the 'Principles Relating to the Status of Commissions and their Advisory Role -, were in the first place geared towards human rights commissions, not towards the broad category of NHRIs as understood today. Secondly, the identification of NHRIs today is much influenced by considerations and interests of different organisational gatekeepers. The ICC has adopted its own interpretation of the Paris Principles in the SCA General Observations and ICC accreditation allows for an up-to-date and straightforward identification of relatively reliable NHRIs. In addition, ICC accreditation is carried out under the auspices of the OHCHR, and is thus intrinsically embedded in the UN human rights system. Last, but not least, the risk is real to get 'lost in translation'. This would be the case when varying interpretations of different organisational gatekeepers would be applicable to the same national body in the same circumstances. In view of the ultimate goal to enhance the promotion and protection of human rights across the world, it should be considered a matter of priority to ensure that the varying supranational approaches towards NHRIs are conducted in a compatible and mutually conducive manner.

Thus, it is the practice and performance of the institution that determines its effectiveness, and the perception that the people have of its working within the state as well as internationally. The International Council on Human Rights and Policy (ICHRP) has identified eleven indices against which the effectiveness of NHRIs can be measured. NHRIs are effective if they enjoy public legitimacy; are accessible; have an open organisational culture; ensure the integrity and quality of their members; consult with civil society; have a broad mandate; have an all-encompassing jurisdiction; have the power to monitor the compliance of their recommendations; treat human rights issues systemically; have adequate budgetary resources; and develop international links. As regards the NHRIs that are authorised to handle individual complaints, they should handlethem speedily and effectively.

However, Implementation of International Human Rights law standards depends largely on the voluntary compliance by the states. Hence, the most effective way to implement Human Rights vests within the legal systems of the different states. Domestic law of a state is required to provide an effective system of remedies for violations of International Human Rights obligations. International law has not become that strong so as to enforce and implement Human Rights violations committed by a state.

But considerable point is, the NHRIs make recommendations to government, which include: payment of compensation to the victim or to her/his family; disciplinary proceedings against delinquent officials; the registration of criminal cases against those responsible; instructions to take particular action to protect human rights and/or to refrain from actions that violate human rights. However, they can only make recommendations, without the power to enforce decisions. This lack of authority to ensure compliance has unfortunate consequences:

- **Outright rejection of a recommendation**:

Governments often ignore the recommendation completely or furnish a long bureaucratic discourse on how compliance with the reommendation is not in the public interest.

- **Partial compliance**:

An example of this is a failure to release the full amount of compensation. Another example is to take action on only one recommendation when there were actually dual recommendations, such as to pay compensation and take disciplinary action.

- **Delayed compliance**:

While recommendations usually obligate governments to take action within 4-6 weeks, compliance is rare within the stipulated time and sometimes action is so delayed that it becomes meaningless.

The National Human Rights Institutions are thus deficient and dependent in many respects. Even after many decades of their inception, they are struggling to establish themselves as autonomous and effective human right institutions, as envisaged by the Paris Principles. The inherent weaknesses and inadequacies of their empowering legislation urgently need to be reformed. These are too important institutions to be neglected. So, after analyzing the functioning of NHRIs in terms of domestic and international perspective, following suggestions can be given which will make the NHRIs strong, independent and vibrant institutions protecting various human rights and will ensure the efficacy and efficiency of Human Rights enforcement machinery and would go a long way in realising the goal of protection and promotion of human rights.

- First of all, the effectiveness of the NHRIs will be greatly enhanced if their recommendations are immediately made enforceable by the government. This will save considerable time and energy as NHRIs will no longer need to either send reminders to government departments to implement the recommendations or alternatively to approach High Courts through a cumbersome judicial process to make the government take action. NHRIs must also have clear and well-defined powers to proceed against government departments

furnishing false reports. This will assist in preventing the many instances where the departmental version of events is more often than not a white-wash, particularly in those cases where the police has been accused of violations.
- Their is urgent need to Include armed forces in the ambit of the NHRIs. A large number of human rights violations occur in areas where there is insurgency and internal conflict. Not allowing NHRIs to independently investigate complaints against the military and security forces only compounds the problems and furthers cultures of impunity. It is essential that commissions are able to summons witnesses and documents, rather than the present situation where the NHRIs are restricted to seeking reports from the national Government.
- NHRIs' membership is also a great matter of concern. As non-judicial member positions are increasingly being filled by ex-bureaucrats, credence is given to the contention that NHRIs are more an extension of the government, rather than independent agencies exercising oversight. If NHRIs are to play a meaningful role in society, they must include civil society human rights activists as members. Many activists have the knowledge and on-the-ground experience of contemporary trends in the human rights movement to be an asset to the NHRIs.
- Independent recruitment of staff has also become need of the hour. Human rights institutions need to develop an independent cadre of staff with appropriate experience. The present arrangement of having to reply on those on deputation from different government departments is not satisfactory as experience has shown that most have little knowledge and understanding of human rights issues. This problem can be rectified by employing specially recruited and qualified staff to help clear the heavy inflow of complaints.

- The NHRIs also need a separate agency to investigate police-related complaints. Experience has shown time and again that complaints regarding police excesses and misbehaviour take up most of the time of human rights institutions. It is perhaps time to think about an alternative agency, dedicated solely to civilian oversight of the police. Here we can learn from international experience: the UK, for instance, has an Independent Police Complaints Commission; South Africa has an Independent Complaints Directorate; and Brazil has Police Ombudsmen offices is some provinces to deal exclusively with police complaints.
- The regional offices have to be established for the NHRIs for the convenience of the general public. Alternatively, Human Rights Standing Committees may be constituted in all Panchayats, Municipalities and Corporations.
- The National Human Rights institutions may be empowered to observe the decisions of the Supreme Court protecting Human Rights and any failure in the implementation of the decision may be brought before the Judiciary for adequate action.
- A new Ministry of Human Rights should be created both at the central and state levels, for effective promotion and protection of Human Rights. This Ministry would help the government to discharge its various duties relating to Human Rights protection effectively.
- The judicial innovation of Public Interest Litigation should now be incorporated into the Constitution itself to make it wide ranging and authoritative for enforcement.
- The right to compensation for violations of Human Rights should be recognised as fundamental right and it should be incorporated in the Constitutions of the countries.
- National Constitutions should be amended so as to include

all Human Rights strictly in accordance with the changing scenario of International Human Rights law.
- At international level there is urgent need that firstly, an International Human Rights law commission should be created through which new Human Rights should be identified and made accessible to individuals. Therefore International Covenants should be strengthened on the recommendations of the International Human Rights Law Commission. The members of the International Human Rights law commission should be elected by the members of the General Assembly. The commission should have coordination with the National Human Rights Institutions for effective promotion and protection of Human Rights. Secondly, an International Court of Human Rights should be established. Due to the formation of number of conventions relating to Human Rights and thereby generating International Human Rights Law, there is an urgent need to interpret this. Therefore an independent court of Human Rights should be created to which individuals and group of individuals would have access by way of appeals, if available domestic remedies have been exhausted.

While these suggestions would help bring about qualitative improvement, the challenge lies in moving the government to accept these and other progressive ideas. Governments across the world are only too keen on maintaining the status quo. Governments often put in place inadequate accountability mechanisms as their presence helps to silence public demands, without overly diluting government power. If these concerns are addressed, the NHRIs will certainly raise the protection and promotion of human rights to a higher level. However, this will only be possible if the respective authorities have the will to respect the institutions' autonomy, thus enhancing their credibility and effectiveness.

Civil society groups therefore need to mobilise people across the world through targeted advocacy strategies. Reform initiatives can only bear fruit when ordinary citizens take an active interest in good governance and human rights. These suggestions if implemented, will certainly go a long way in realising the cherished goal "All Human Rights to All".

BIBLIOGRAPHY
A. PRIMARY SOURCES
(i) Judicial Cases of India

A.D.M. Jabalpur v. Shivkant Shukla, AIR 1976 SC 1207

Bandhua Mukti Morcha v Union of India, AIR 1984 SC, 80A

Chairman Railway Board V: Chandrimadas, AIR. 2000 S.C. 988

Chintaman Rao v. State of MP, 1950 SCR 759

D.K.B. Basu v State of West Bengal, AIR. 1997 S.C. 610

Darshan Singh v. State of Punjab and Ors., AIR 2010 SC 1212

Extra Judicial Execution Victim Families Association(EEVFAM) and Ors. v. Union of India and Ors., AIR 2016 SC 3400,

Francis Coralie v. Union Territory Delhi, A.I.R. 1981 S.C. 746

Golak Nath v State of Punjab, AIR. 1967 S.C. p. 211

Hussainara Khatoon v. Home Secretary, State of Bihar, AI.R. 1979 S.C. 1360

Indian Express Newspaper v. Union of India, (1985) 1 SC, 64

Jolly George Varghese v. The Bank of Cochin,. A.I.R. 1980 S.C. 470

Keshvanand Bharti v. State of Kerala, AI.R. 1973 S.C., 1461

Laxmi v. State of UP, AIR 1981 SC 873,

Maneka Gandhi v. Union of India, AIR. 1978 S.C. 597

Mullus Hospital v. Member Secretary, AIR 2004 Kant. 342

National Human Rights Commission v State of Arunachal Pradesh and another,(1966) 1 SCC 742

Olga Tellis v. Bombay Municipal Corporation, A.I.R. 1986 S.C. 180

Paramjeet Kaur v. State of Punjab, (1991) 2 SCC 131

People's Union for Civil Liberties and another v. State of Maharastra, 2015 CrLJ 610

Qureshi v. State of Bihar, 193 9CR 62%,

Rudalshah v State of Bihar, A.IR. 1983 S.C. 1086

Ramkrishna Dalmia v. Justice Tendulakar, AIR 1958 SC 538

State of West Bengal v. Shbodh Gopal Bose, AIR 1954 SC 92-96

Sheela Barse v. State of Maharashtra, A.I.R. 1983 S.C. 378

Tukaram v. State of Maharashtra, (1979) 2 SCC 143

Upendra Baxi v U.O.I (1983) 2 S.C.C. 309

Vishakha and Others v State of Rajasthan and Others, AIR 1997 (6) 5CC 241

Zahira Habibulla v. Sheikh & An. a State of Gujarat & Ors., 2004 5CC

(ii) Reports and Government Documents of India

- A Guide to the Protection of Human Rights Act, 1993.
- A Handbook on the Establishment and Strengthening of National Institutions for the Promotion and Protection of Human Rights, Professional Training Series No. 4, Centre for Human Rights, Geneva, 1995.
- Annual Reports of the NHRC of India, 1993-94, 1994-95, 1995-96, 1996-97, 1997-98,1998-99, 1999-2000, 2000-01, 2001-02, 2002-03, 2003-04, 2004-05, 2005-06,2006-07, 2007-08, 2008-09., 2009-10, 2010-11, 2011-12, 2012-13.
- Canadian Human Rights Foundation, Annual Report, 2005.
- Commonwealth of Human Rights Initiative, Newsletter, vol. 2, no. 5, New Delhi, 1996.
- Compliance Manual of Canadian Human Rights Commission, 2007.
- News Letter, Human Rights, Vol. 12 No-11, Nov., 2015 NHRC.
- News Letter, Human Rights, Vol. 12 No-12, Dec., 2015 NHRC.
- News Letter, Human Rights, Vol. 12 No-7, July, 2015 NHRC.
- News Letter, Human Rights, Vol. 12 No-8, August, 2015 NHRC.
- News Letter, Human Rights, Vol. 12 No-9, Sept., 2015

NHRC.
- News Letter, Human Rights, Vol. 13 No-2, Feb., 2016 NHRC.
- News Letter, Human Rights, Vol. 13 No-4, April, 2016 NHRC.
- News Letter, Human Rights, Vol. 14 No-11, Nov., 2016 NHRC.
- News Letter, Human Rights, Vol. 14 No-12, Dec, 2016 NHRC.
- News Letter, Human Rights, Vol. 14 No-5, May, 2016 NHRC.
- News Letter, Human Rights, Vol. 14 No-6, June, 2016 NHRC.
- News Letter, Human Rights, Vol. 14 No-7, July, 2016 NHRC.
- News Letter, Human Rights, Vol. 14 No-9, Sept., 2016 NHRC.
- News Letter, Human Rights, Vol. 14 No-1, January, 2017 NHRC.
- News Letter, Human Rights, Vol. 14 No-2, February, 2017 NHRC.

B. SECONDARY SOURCES
Books

- Agarwal R.S., Human Rights in the Modern World, New Delhi: CI Publications,1983.
- Austin G., The Indian Constitution—The Cornerstone of a Nation, Oxford University Press, 1996.
- Bajwa G.S., Human Rights in India: Implementation and Violation, New Delhi:Anmol Publications, 1995.
- Chand A., Politics of Human Rights and Civil Liberties: A Global Survey, Delhi:U.B.H. Publishers, 1985.

- Chandra A., Human Rights Activism and Role of NGO's, New Delhi: Rajat Publications,2000.
- David B., (ed.), Politics and Human Rights, Oxford: Blackwell Publishers, 1995.
- Desai A.R., Violation of Democratic Rights in India, Bombay: Popular Prakashan,1986.
- Diwan P. and Peeyushi Diwan, Human Rights in India, Deep and Deep Publications,New Delhi, 1996.
- Jha K.C., Resurrecting Human Rights in India, New Delhi: Shriden Book Company,1995.
- Jøhari J.C., Human Rights and New World Order Toward the Perfection of the
- Democratic Way of Life, New Delhi: Anmol Publications, 1996.
- Karkara G.S., Commentary on the Protection of Human Rights Act, 1993, Jaipur:
- Dominion Law Depot, 2003.
- Mani V.S., Human Rights in India: A Survey, in K.P. Saksena, ed., Human Rights:Fifty Years of India's Independence (New Delhi, 1999).
- Mohapatra A.R., National Human Rights Commission of India Formation,Functioning and Future Prospectus, New Delhi: Radha Publications, 2001.
- Saksena K.P., Human Rights and the Constitution Vision and the Reality, New Delhi:Gyan Publishing House, 2003.
- Saksena K.P., Human Rights: Perspective and Challenges, New Delhi: Lancers Books, 1994.
- Taneja S.L., Analysis of the Provisions of the Protection of Human Rights Act, 1993:A View Point, 2000.
- Tony E., The Politics of Human Rights: A Global Perspective, London: Pluto Press,2001.
- Vincent R.J., Human Rights and International Relations,

Cambridge: CambridgeUniversity Press, 1986.
- Waldron J., Human Rights and the Search for Community Consciousness, London: The Oxford Amnesty Lecturers, 1992.
- Younghusband F.E., South Africa of Today, London: Macmillan & Company, 1899.
- Zuberi T., Sibanda and E. Udjo, The Demography of South Africa, New York, M.E.
- Sharpe, 2005.

(ii) Journals and Periodicals

- Ahmadi A.M., Inaugural Speech at a Workshop on Judicial Process, Social
- Legitimacy and Institutional Viability, The Institute of Advanced Legal Studies,Pune, December 16, 1995.
- Anand A.S., Protection of Human Rights: Judicial Obligation or Judicial Activism (1997) 7 SCC (Journal Section) at page 11.
- Annual Report on the Work of Organization, New York, 1999), pp. 16, para 53.
- Azad S.A.K., Indian Judiciary: A Saviour of Life and Personal Liberty, A.I.R. 2000 (Journal Section) 17.
- Baxi U., Sins of Commission Link, May 1993, p. 51.
- Bhagwati P.N., Enforcement of Fundamental Rights: Role of Courts, Paper presented at Judicial Colloquium in Bangalore, February, 1988.
- Bishrtoi B.R., Role of the National Human Rights Commission Towards Human Rights Literacy and Awareness, 2005 (3) RDD 21 (Journal).
- Chandrasekharan K.N., Protection of Human Rights: A Review of the Enforcement
- Machinery in India, the Academy Law Review, Volume

XXIII (1999).
- Chhibar Y.P., National Human Rights Commission; A View from People's Front (in K.P. Saksena, ed.) note 23, (2000).
- Das H.B., Human Rights-A Dicta of a Civilized Society, note a Mere Constitutional Guarantee, A.I.R. 2004 (Jounral Section) 60.
- Dayal V., Statement at 52nd Session of the United Nations Commission on Human Rights at Geneva, 10 April, 1996.
- Gupta J.P., Emerging Socio-Economic Trends: Role of Lawyers and Legal Institutions, A.I.R. 1999 (Journal Section) 175.
- Jain S., Changing Methods of Warfare and Violations of Human Rights of Civilians, A.I.R. 2005 (Journal Section) 17.
- Katju M., The Significance of Human Rights and Its Co-Relation with Judicial Functioning, AIR. 2003 (Journal Section) 228.
- Khanna H.R., Human Rights: Dimension and Challenges, AIR. 1998 (Journal Section) 49.
- Mathur R.N., Human Rights and Role of NHRC, A Paper Presented at the Seminar on Human Rights Education, Jointly Organised by the CHRC and NHRC, 16 February, 1996, New Delhi.
- Pillai R.V., Human Rights Training for National Institutions, A Paper Presented at the Seminar on Human Rights Education, Jointly organised by the Canadian Human Rights Commission and the National Human Rights Commission, 16 February, 1996, New Delhi.
- Saxena K.P., Human Rights and Equal Opportunity, Lecture Delivered at Institute of World Congress on Human Rights, 22nd March, 1996.
- Sharma R.P., Human Rights: An Overview, AIR 2003,

(Journal Section) 65.
- Shiviah M., Human Rights and the Third World: towards a Reassessment of Ideological Dynamics, Economic and Political Weekly, 18 Nov. 1995,
- pp. 2937-46. Singh A.P., Human Rights: The Indian Context, A.I.R. 200O (Journal Section) 8..
- Singh D., Human Rights in India - A Captive Commission? Sikh Review, Vol. 41, No. 472 (1993) page 44.

- **Websites**

http://nhrc.nic.in/Publications/NHRCbrochure.pdf

http://nhrc.nic.in/Publications/HRActEng.pdf

http://www.thehindu.com/news/national/article995690.ece

www.dnaindia.com/india/report_sc-seeks-status-report-about-action-against-nhrcchief_1649494

ibnlive.in.com/news/what-is-the-salwa-judum/165206-3.html

articles.timesofindia.indiatimes.com > Collections

www.ensaaf.org/programs/legal/pmc/

www.alrc.net/PDF/HRActEng.pdf

india.gov.in/spotlight/spotlight_archive.php?id=73

www.nhrc.nic.in/.../NHRC_Comments_on_AiNNI_Report.pdf

nhrc.nic.in/disparchive.asp?fno=874

ACRONYMS

ADR : Alternative Dispute Resolution/Alternative Dispute Resolution
AI : Amnesty International
AIDS : Acquired Immunodeficiency Syndrome
AIR : All India Reports
APCL : Andhra Pradesh Civil Liberty
APT : Association for the Prevention of Torture
AWID : Association for Women's Rights in Development
CASE : Community Agency for Social Enquiry
CAT : Convention against Torture and Other Cruel, Inhuman or Degrading Treatment or punishment/Committee against Torture
CBCI : Catholic Bishops Conference of India
CBCID : Crime Branch Central Investigation Department
CCA : Common Country Assessment
CEDAW : Convention on the Elimination of All Forms of Discrimination against Women
CESCR : Committee on Economic, Social and Cultural Rights
CGE : Commission for Gender Equality
CJ : Chief Justice
CrPC : Criminal Procedure Code
CRPF : Central Revere Police Force
CSOS : Civil Society Organisations
DDO : Drawing and Disbursing Officer
DRC : Development Resource Centre
ECOWAS : Economic Community of Western African States

ECOWAS : Economic Community of West African States
FR : Fundamental Right(s)
HC : High Court
HIV : Human Immunodeficiency Virus
HRA : Human Rights Association
HRC : Human Rights Cell/Human Right Court
HRCA : Human Rights Commission Act
ICC : International Criminal Court
ICCR : International Covenant on Civil and Political Rights
ICESCR : International Covenant on Economic, Social and Cultural Rights
ICNL : International Center for Not-Profit Law
IDP : Internally Displaced Person
IEC : The Independent Election Commission
INC : Indian National Congress
IO : Investigating Officer
IOI : International Ombudsman Institute
IPC : Indian Penal Code
IPRO : Indian Public Relation Officer
IR : Informal Resolution
KBK : Kalahandi, Bolangir and Koraput,
MDG : Millennium Development Goal
MKSS : The Mazdoor Kisan Shakti Sangathan
MTCT : Mother-to-child-transmission
NCW : National Commission for Women
NGO : Non-Governmental Organisation
NHRC : National Human Rights Commission
NHRIs : National Human Rights Institutions
NIC : National Informatics Centre
NPCIS : News Paper Clipping Information System
PAIA : Promotion of access to Information Act, 2 of 2000.
PDS : Public Distribution System

PEPUDA : Promotion of Equality and Prevention of Unfair Discrimination Act
POTA : Prevention of Terrorism Act
PUCL : Peoples Union of Civil Liberty
PUCLDR : People's Union for Civil Liberties and Democratic Rights
PUDR : People's Union for Democratic Rights
RAF : Rapid Acton Force
RTI : Right to Information Act, 2005
SC : Scheduled Caste/Supreme Court
SCA : The Supreme Court of Appeal
SCC : Supreme Court Cases
SCR : Supreme Court Reports
SG : Secretary General
SPOs : Special police Officers
ST : Scheduled Tribes
TAC : Treatment Action Campaign
TRC : Truth and Reconciliation Commission
UHRC : Uganda Human Rights Commission
UN : United Nations
UNDP : United Nations Development Programme
UPR : Universal Periodic Review
VHP : Vishwa Hindu Parishad
WG : Working Group

---

[1] The Universal Declaration of Human Rights, 1948, Article 1.

[2] Alexander Hamilton in Preface of his book on Human Rights, 1st Edition 1775.

[3] National, institutions for the promotion and protection of human rights. (accessed online 13 June 2012 on http:// www. Unhcr .ch/html/menu6/2/fs 19.htm.)

[4] Brian Burdekin and Anne Gallagher, 'The United Nations and National Human Rights Institutions', Human Rights-2/1998, A Quarterly Review of the Office of the UN High Commissioner for Human Rights, P.21.

[5] Cardenas, S Adaptive State: The proliferation of national human rights institutions (accessed online- http://www.ksq.harvard.edu/cchrp/web%20working%20papers/cardenas.pdf.).

[6] Burdekin, B and Evans, C National Human rights institutions: A global trend" Canadian Human Rights Foundation newsletter. 2000 Volume XV; No. 2 1

[7] Centre of Human Rights Professional Training Series No. 4 National Human Rights Institutions: A Handbook on the Establishment and strengthening of national institutions for the promotion and protection of human rights (UN Handbook) 6.

[8] The Universal Declaration of Human Rights, 1948.

[9] The international Covenant on Civil and Political Rights and the International Covenant on Economic, Social and Cultural (ESC) Rights adopted by the UN Assembly in 1966 and came into force from 23rd March, 1976 and 3rd Jan., 1976 respectively.

[10] The Convention on Rights of the Child, 1989 and the Articles on Discrimination against Women.

[11] As per figures estimated by UNESCO, July 2002.

[12] Carver, R and Hunt, P "National Human Rights Institutions. In Africa" in Hossain (n1 above) 733.

[13] Burdekin, B and Evans, C National Human rights institutions: A global trend" Canadian Human Rights Foundation newsletter. 2000 Volume XV; No. 2 1

[14] Principles relating to the status and functioning of national human rights institutions for the protection and promotion of human rights. http:// www. Unhchr. Ch/html/menu6/2/fs 19.htm. (accessed on 20 June 2014)

[15] Second Article of the Paris Principles.

[16] For Example: ICC Comment on Interference by government - "The ICC[1] Sub-Committee on Accreditation's commented on Ireland's NHRI[2] in November 2008: "IHRC should be able to independently conduct its affairs without undue interference from the Government. This could include having direct accountability to Parliament"

[17] CHR (2008). "Business and Human Rights: A Survey of NHRI Practices. Results from a survey distributed by the Office of [3]OH[4]the United Nations High Commissioner for Human Rights."[5]

[18] ICC Sub-Committee on Accreditation General Observations (Geneva, June 2009)[6].

[19] An example of such institutions is the Ugandan Human Rights Commission (UHRC).

[20] UNHRC 1992/54. 1992; General Assembly Resolution 48/138, 1993.

[21] UN Handbook.

[22] For example a project, entitled 'Action Research Study on the Institutional Development of Human Rights in Bangladesh' (IDHRB) was undertaken by the UNDP to assess the need of establishing the NHRC.

[23] K.P Saksena, Human Rights: Perspective and Challenges, New Delhi, Lancers Books (1994) at P. 23

[24] The fourteen States are: Assam, Chattisgarh, Himachal Pradesh, Jammu & Kashmir, Kerala, Madhya Pradesh, Maharashtra, Manipur, Orissa, Punjab, Rajasthan, Tamil Nadu, Uttar Pradesh, West Bengal, Karnataka, Uttrakhand, Andhrapradesh, Gujarat, Jharkhan, Haryana, bihar, goa, sikkim and tripura. See http:nhrc.in

---

1. http://www.ohchr.org/en/countries/nhri/pages/nhrimain.aspx
2. http://www.ihrc.ie/
3. http://w02.unssc.org/free_resources/UNDP-OHCHRToolkit/pdf/2008.doc
4. http://w02.unssc.org/free_resources/UNDP-OHCHRToolkit/pdf/2008.doc
5. http://w02.unssc.org/free_resources/UNDP-OHCHRToolkit/pdf/2008.doc
6. http://w02.unssc.org/free_resources/UNDP-OHCHRToolkit/pdf/June-English.pdf

[25] See for details. The Protection of Human Rights Act 1993 with Procedural Regulations.

[26] Section 3 of the Protection of Human Rights Act, 1993.

[27] Section 12(a)(i) and (ii) of the Act.

[28] section 4 of the Act.

[29] Section 2 (d) of the Protection of Human Rights Act, 1993.

[30] Articles 38 to 51-A contain the Directive Principles of State Policy. The idea to have such principles in the Constitution has been borrowed from the Irish Constitution. The Directive Principles are not enforceable by the Court.

[31] India ratified both instruments on 10 April 1979.

[32] D.D.Basu, Thunan Rights in Constitutional Law (New Delhi, Prentice Hall. 1994).

[33] Gurjeet Singh, Role of National Institutions and Non-Governmental Organizations in the Promotion and Protection of Human Rights (2001).

[34] Rajendra Prasad Saxena, Human Rights Movements in India and National Human Rights Commission (1999) at page 141.

[35] under Sections 18 and 19 of the Act.

[36] Programmes and Perspectives of NHRC (2001) at page 124.

[37] Section 12 of the protection of Human Rights Act, 1993.

[38] Secs. 21 and 30 of the Protection of Human Rights Act of 1993.

[39] B.V. Somasekher, Programmes and Perspective of NHRC Towards Protection of Human Rights in India: An Appraisal (2001) at pages 552-53.

[40] The fourteen States are: Assam, Chattisgarh, Himachal Pradesh, Jammu & Kashmir, Kerala, Madhya Pradesh, Maharashtra, Manipur, Orissa, Punjab, Rajasthan, Tamil Nadu, Uttar Pradesh, West Bengal, Karnataka, Uttrakhand, Andhrapradesh, Gujarat, Jharkhand, Haryana, bihar, goa, sikkim and tripura. See http:nhrc.in

[41] Ibid, at page 31.

[42] OHCHR, "Survey of national human rights institutions: report on the findings and recommendations of a questionnaire addressed to NHRIs worldwide", 2009, available online www.nhri.net.

[43] A.I.R. 1973 S.C. 1461 at 1510.

[44] A.I.R. 1980S.C.4708.474.

[45] A comparative analysis bases on the theoritial provisions of both the documents.

[46] A.I.R. 2000 (I) S.C. 265,

[47] A.I.R. 1976 S.C. 1207 at 1293

[48] A.I.R. 1967 S.C. 1643 at 1656

[49] A.I.R. 1973 S.C. 1461 at 1536.

[50] A.I.R. 1954 S.C. 92 at 96.

[51] Steps towards protection and promotion of human rights, Achivements of NHRC-Vol-I, Page 9, Published by NHRC.

[52] Complicated encounters –Doval, Ajit Kumar - The Indian Express, Aug 04 2010.

[53] Most Police encounters-2016, The Wire, 21-10-2016.

[54] Mannual on human rights for Police Officers, Page 24, Punlished by NHRC.

[55] AIR 2016 SC 3400.

[56] AIR 2010 SC 1212.

[57] D.O. letter No.4/7/2008-PRP&P.

[58] 2015 CriLJ 610.

[59] Mannual on human rights for Police Officers, Page 26, Punlished by NHRC.

[60] Article 9.

[61] Article 14.

[62] Princliple 35.

[63] Case No. 3177/96-97/NHRC, Source: NHRC Annual Report 1998-99.

[64] AIR 1997 SC 610.

[65] Rreport sent to the UN mandated HRCfor the third Universal Periodic Review by the NHRC.

[66] 2001-2002 Annual Report of the national Human Rights Commission

[67] 2002-2003 Annual Report of the national Human Rights Commission

[68] 2003-2004 Annual Report of the national Human Rights Commission

[69] 2004-2005 Annual Report of the national Human Rights Commission

[70] 2005-2006 Annual Report of the national Human Rights Commission

[71] 2006-2007 Annual Report of the national Human Rights Commission

[72] 2007-2008 Annual Report of the national Human Rights Commission

[73] 2008-2009 Annual Report of the national Human Rights Commission

[74] NHRC Case no. 23/2/10/2010-AD.

[75] NHRC Case no. 23/2/10/2010-AD.

[76] NHRC Case no. 7/15/2/2010/UC/M5.

[77] NHRC Case No. 6/15/3/2010-AD.

[78] under Article 136 of the Constitution of India.

[79] As per recently released data by the National Crime Records Bureau (NCRB) on its official website.

[80] Article 21-A of the Constitution of India.

[81] Article 22 of the Constitution of India.

[82] Except where one is arrested under a preventive detention law

[83] Article 23 and 24 of the Constitution of India.

[84] Article 25 of the Constitution of India.

[85] Article 26 of the Constitution of India.

[86] Article 27 of the Constitution of India.

[87] Article 28 of the Constitution of India.

[88] Article 29 of the Constitution of India.

[89] Article 30 of the Constitution of India.

[90] Article 32 of the Constitution of India.

[91] Article 32(2) of the Constitution of India.

[92] Article 226 of the Constitution of India.

[93] Under Article 13 of the Constitution of India.

[94] Under Article 141 of the Constitution of India.

[95] Under Part-IV of the Constitution of In

[96] Under Article 37 of the Constitution of In

[97] Kamlaker V. State of Maharashtra, 2004 (1) All India CF.L.R 122

[98] Article 38 of the Constitution of India.

[99] Article 39(a) of the Constitution of India.

[100] Article 39(b) of the Constitution of India.

[101] Article 39(c) of the Constitution of India.

[102] Article 39(d) of the Constitution of India.

[103] Article 39(e) of the Constitution of India.

[104] Article 39(f) of the Constitution of India.

[105] Article 39(g) of the Constitution of India.

[106] Article 40 of the Constitution of India.

[107] Article 41 of the Constitution of India.

[108] Article 42 of the Constitution of India.

[109] Article 43 of the Constitution of India.

[110] Article 43-A of the Constitution of India.

[111] Article 44 of the Constitution of India.

[112] Article 45 of the Constitution of India.

[113] Article 46 of the Constitution of India.

[114] Article 47 of the Constitution of India.

[115] Article 48 of the Constitution of India.

[116] Article 49 of the Constitution of India.

[117] Article 50 of the Constitution of India.

[118] Article 51 of the Constitution of India.

[119] Case No.37/3/97-LD(FC).

[120] 30/3/2003-2004-AF.

[121] Ref: 1/1997/NHRC.

[122] Case No. 41/9/2004-2005.

[123] Case No. 736/19/2003-2004.

[124] Paramjit Kaur v State of Punjab (1999) 2 SCC 131.

[125] (1999) 2 SCC 131.

[126] Committee on the elimination of all forms of discrimination against women, 1992, general recommendation 19.

[127] Case No. 1172/30/9/09-10-AR reported in the Annual Report 2009-10 of the Commission.

[128] Case No. 52571/24/43/07-08-PF published in the Annual report of the Commission.

[129] Case No. 658/01/2006-07-WC reported in the Annual Report 2006-07 of the Commission.

[130] Sama 2005: Advancing Right to Health: Indian Cotext: page 5.

[131] Kapilashrami, Anuj (2006) 'Women's Health: A Decade of Skewed Priorities' in From Shadows to Self- NGO Country Report 2005: Beijing +10, India Women's Watch.

[132] Case No. 72/27/2006-07-WC reported in the Annual Report 2006-07 of the Commission.

[133]

Source: www.nhrc.nic.in

[134]

UN Doc. E/CN.4/1992/23, 14 February 1992.

[135] UN Office of the High Commissioner for Human Rights (OHCHR), National Human Rights Institutions: History, Principles, Roles and Responsibilities, Professional Training Series No. 4 (Rev. 1) (2010) 13.

About the Author

The author is a Law Professor and former Legal practitionerand has fair amount of educational and professional eperience.The Author has completed her master of laws (LL.M.) in Constitutional Laws and Master of Philosophy (M.Phil) and Doctor of Philosophy (Ph.D.) degrees in law and human rights. The author possesses good fundamental knowledge of national and international legal obligations on various issues like the present dealt in this book.

www.ingramcontent.com/pod-product-compliance
Lightning Source LLC
Chambersburg PA
CBHW052302220526
45471CB00001B/446